"As a single gal, I jumped for joy at a cookbook that is all about making food for one person. Y'all know how many carrots I killed cuz I couldn't eat/use them fast enough? A LOT! Anyway, Meredith's wit and easy-to-follow recipes make cooking loads of fun and delicious. Also, this book is cute as hell! Even if you're not in the mood to cook, you'll wanna chill on your couch and just flip through this book! It's a win-win!"

—Phoebe Robinson, *New York Times* bestselling author of *Please Don't Sit on My Bed in Your Outside Clothes* and actress

"As a connoisseur of cooking shows, cookbooks, and single-serve recipes that don't require an abacus, I am excited to be invited to *Party for One*. In her clever, accessible, and delightfully down-to-earth offering, Meredith Dawson welcomes each of us to enjoy the art of dining alone without being lonely. From salty snacks and hearty mains to craveable desserts, she has written a winner—and a lifesaver."

—Stacey Abrams, *New York Times* bestselling author of *While Justice Sleeps*, producer, and political leader

"If only I'd had this book when I was single. Having spent way too much money eating out because all the recipes I had served four people, *Party for One* would have been a godsend. Meredith's dishes are delicious, her writing is tons of fun, and you'll have lots of extra room in your now leftovers-less fridge. Happy cooking!"

—Paul Feig, author of *Cocktail Time: The Ultimate Guide to Grown Up Fun* and filmmaker

Party for One

Party for One

Perfectly Portioned Recipes Just for You

Meredith Dawson

with Emily Stephenson

Photographs by
Ghazalle Badiozamani

Union Square & Co.
Hachette Book Group
1290 Avenue of the Americas, New York, NY 10104
unionsquareandco.com
@unionsqandco

First Edition: May 2026

Union Square & Co. is an imprint of Grand Central Publishing, a division of Hachette Book Group, Inc. The Union Square & Co. name and logo are registered trademarks of Hachette Book Group, Inc.

Editors: Caitlin Leffel and Amanda Englander
Designer: Renée Bollier with contributing interior design by Baseball Diamond
Photographer: Ghazalle Badiozamani
Food Stylist: Barrett Washburne
Prop Stylist: Megan Hedgpeth
Project Editor: Donna Wright
Production Manager: Kevin Iwano
Copy Editor: Ivy McFadden

Library of Congress Control Number has been applied for.

ISBNs 978-1-4549-5882-6 (hardcover), 978-1-4549-5883-3 (ebook)

Printed in China

1010

10 9 8 7 6 5 4 3 2 1

This cookbook is dedicated to my future life partner. Should we meet, fall in love, and live happily ever after, please know I will continue making my single servings and you will be on your own for dinner. *xo*

Contents

Sizzled & Crisp 110

Spicy & Hot 156

Glazy & Saucy 136

Nice & Sweet 174

Nutrition Facts
Calories 30

Introduction

Have you ever had a rough day and the only thing that will soothe your sadness is a single warm, gooey chocolate chip cookie? Perhaps you've stumbled upon a fabulous recipe for lasagna, but you don't have seven people at your beck and call to share it with. Or maybe you're the type of person who can't stand eating leftovers more than once a week. Or MAYBE, dare I say, you were gifted fine Canadian maple syrup and are craving French toast, but you know all the recipes available to you will leave you with a stack of extra toast you'll simply never eat? Maybe you're a hungry baller living on your own, a hungry empty nester, a hungry divorcée, a hungry widower getting your groove back, a hungry college student . . . Each of those scenarios would benefit from a cookbook that offers this solution: **single servings**.

The two words that best describe me are *determined* and *hungry*. I can be obsessive, and when I want something, my brain will accelerate into overdrive until I get it or have exhausted every option trying to get it. It's great for work (sometimes) but bad when you have a nasty sweet tooth. At 9 p.m. on the dot, an alarm in my brain goes off that tells me I must eat something sweet. And not like an Oreo. I need fresh cake. Or a fresh cookie. And so one night during the 2020 COVID pandemic, I was in the middle of writing a difficult scene for a movie script and couldn't figure out how to end this pivotal moment—we're talking big-swelling-music, guy-finally-gets-the-girl, third-act kinda stuff. I rolled myself down on the floor to moan and bask in self-pity, as one does, and after some light sorrow and despair, the solution magically appeared. I jumped up and finished the scene. It was a triumph. It was incredible. It was also 9 p.m. and I needed sugar. I ransacked my cupboards looking for my reward, but there was nothing! Not even a crumb of something sweet. Two hours later, I had a fresh batch of two dozen sugar cookies. After eating six of them, I felt ill, and even worse, I felt guilty knowing I would have to eat all those stupid cookies over the rest of the week because I didn't have the heart to throw them out. So while no longer hungry, I thought, *This is a terrible state of affairs*, and became determined to write a different script for myself when I felt hungry—I decided to write a cookbook! If that has ever happened to you (my God, why would it????), then this book is something you'll also appreciate. This book is for the people who have a craving and need to satisfy it, but in moderation!

Speaking of things that are sweet and come in chocolate, now's a great time to introduce myself. Hi! I'm Meredith Dawson, the author of this cookbook! I'm originally from the Chicago suburbs but have been grinding, suffering, and sunbathing in Los Angeles since 2012, and recently made the bicoastal move to Brooklyn. I've been professionally writing (aka someone pays me to do it) since 2017 and directing since 2021. I've worked on TV shows you can find on Hulu, Apple TV+, Comedy Central, and Netflix, and written movies that will probably never see the light of day. I'm a comedy writer and my jokes are very funny. I'm also very humble.

I know the irony in saying this, but writing is hard. It's borderline impossible, but one of the best feelings that makes it worth it comes after figuring out a story arc or writing a joke that makes everyone in the room laugh (even if you're the only one in the room). When I meet people who express an interest in writing for TV or film, I tell them it's a great career if they have no other skills and can only think about being a writer. It's a life full of rejection and, well . . . no, it's mostly rejection, but there is something to be said about turning an idea you had on the couch into a tangible object. Credits on TV shows I've written on have of course been screenshotted and shared with friends, but this cookbook is my first tangible object, and I had a delicious time writing it.

"Do you even cook? *Can* you even cook?" That was the response I got when I told people I was writing a cookbook. And that's from the people who *like* me. I can bake, but in their defense, I am an admittedly terrible cook. I don't know how to cut anything the way you're supposed to and I use all my creativity for work. In addition to being a struggling cook, I am also an infrequent one. Or I was, but then the pandemic happened. During the pandemmy, I isolated myself into a "bubble of one," which meant I was eating, sleeping, and entertaining for one. I was never much of a foodie (a result of being lazy and a terrible cook) so I never put much effort into my meals and settled for what was easy. But

I learned very quickly that one can only eat so many Lean Cuisines, so I put on my big-girl pants and cooked. As I went through various websites, articles, and the untouched cookbooks I had on hand, I slowly developed a love and appreciation for cooking. I found myself getting excited to try new things. I wanted to improve my skills and expand my go-to recipes. Despite my progress, there was one thing that always drove me crazy: the serving sizes. And I know I'm not alone. An article featured in *O, The Oprah Magazine* titled "The Power of Dining for One" highlights what it means to take care of yourself, by yourself. Cooking and baking are two of the many things that give us pleasure and allow us to treat ourselves, and treat ourselves we shall. A single serving of something delicious leaves you feeling full, physically and spiritually.

Generally, most recipes are meant to serve four to six people—or more!—but for someone who's by themselves (for whatever reason), that's too much food. As much as I love my Pyrex containers, I don't like making something and then getting stuck with leftovers. I also don't want to waste food. Some websites have the automated capability to scale ingredient quantities for different numbers of servings, but the scaled ingredients often don't make sense. I don't know how to measure .17 of a medium onion or .04 cups of dry red wine. Do you???? Sometimes, there are moments when you just want one thing, but it's not easy to get or it's an unwise use of money. As previously mentioned, I have an insatiable sweet tooth, and every five or so hours, my body is like, "Girl, let's have some cake!" But places that sell individual cookies or cake slices sell them for like seven bucks!!! In this economy???? While my tummy says, "Yes, you deserve this," my brain and wallet say, "Absolutely not, you heathen!" Some grocery stores sell single servings of larger meals, but let's be honest, the food is not always great, and you deserve better. There *should* be an easier way to make what you want in a serving or two, but there aren't many options.

Working as a professional writer, you learn quickly and publicly what your strengths and weaknesses are, and I wasn't going to attempt writing recipes alone. If I did, it would just be the phone number to the nearest Dominos. I worked with smart, cool, great professional developers and testers to help write and test the recipes I wanted, in addition to testing them myself. If I can make everything in this book, I know you can, too!

What *Party for One* brings to the table that's different from other "smaller-portion" cookbooks is not only the recipes, but the tone. I swear, the other day I saw a single-serving cookbook called *You're a Big Single Loser but You Still Have to Eat.* A lot of "smaller-portion" cookbooks are either aimed specifically at couples, conversely seem depressing that they're meant for just for one person, or are rigid, suggesting it's very difficult to cook for one person—whereas I want to **celebrate** cooking for you. While cooking is nurturing and self-care, it's also an opportunity to have fun and celebrate your. Living is hard, and we could all be dead in the morning, so we should eat what we love and love what we eat and, most importantly, not have to eat it every night for a week.

As of the writing of this book, and probably forever, I am single, and my roommate is my dog. I work from home. I am alone 94 percent of the time and . . . dudes, I LOVE IT. I love traveling alone, I love going to the movies alone, and I love going out to dinner alone. Being alone is not the same as being lonely, and the book is titled *Party for One* because making a single thing shouldn't feel sad. The phrase is inspired from when I go out to dinner and the hosts ask if I'm a "party for one." I happily say yes, and then they seat me by the toilets. Which is also why I like to stay in and eat. After a long day of [*insert list of important things that I do during the day*], the last thing I want to do is put my bra and underwear and pants on for the first time, get in my car, drive to a restaurant, park far away/apologize to the valet for all the gum and La Croix cans in my car, and then pay to eat gnocchi I could've made at home. There's also a fine line between staying in but not wanting to order in. Since I'm basically Gordon Ramsay now and like cooking, I want to do it. In fact, most days, I just want to cook one thing and eat that one thing on my couch while watching *Frasier*.

Today's real, modern adult dream is to do things for yourself, by yourself, and be absolutely stoked about it. Baking one or two decadent cookies for yourself should feel like a fun, easy thing, not a daunting, drawn-out process. I want to reframe cooking "because you're alone" to "My husband is at the Dodgers game, and I finally have a night to myself!" or "Huzzah! My roommate is on vacation in the Seychelles with her slam piece, so I don't have to share!" Don't settle for large portions or a dinner you don't want just because it's available. Whether your roommate already ate, you just got your own place, your partner wanted leftovers and you didn't, or you just want what you want, you were correct to choose this book. Eating the single serving of the thing you want is a *luxury*. LEAN INTO IT, BABY! I'm so excited for you to dive in! Blood (literally, I stabbed a knife through my finger testing one of the recipes and needed stitches at urgent care), sweat, tears, and many smoke alarm alerts went into this labor of love. Happy cooking, happy eating, and happy not-leftover-ing!

xo,

Meredith

The Party for One Philosophy

In your typical, everyday, run-of-the-mill cookbook, this is the section where the author (a professional, most likely) waxes poetic about necessary equipment, pantry staples, grocery plans, etc. Well, this is not your typical, everyday, run-of-the-mill cookbook. This is a cookbook written by and for someone with places to be, things to do, and a craving to satisfy. Since you're looking to cook for yourself, you can be more selfish with your time and energy. This is not meal prep, this is not for hosting parties to impress friends, this is not about longevity. This is about you eating in the very near future. I've never met anyone who reads any of the pages before the recipe begins, and honestly, I'm amazed you're even reading this right now. All this to say, my philosophy is to exist at your highest intelligence level and read the entire recipe before you begin. Then you will know what ingredients you'll need, what appliances or equipment you'll be using, and that will be that. The simplest way to cut down on leftovers and eliminate waste is to buy what the recipe asks for, which was a primary consideration that went into developing them. For the unused ingredients, there's a handy-dandy section in the book that will help you look up some of the ingredients to see what else in this book can be made. It's called an index. Use it. There's also the World Wide Web—google it, honey! That being said, there are a few things I'd recommend having on hand, which you can find in the "How to Use This Book" section.

Now stop reading this and get cooking!

How to Use This Book

Okay, oops, a little more to read. Ideally, this is a cookbook you will read in the morning because you obviously keep it in bed with you, find what you want for dinner that night, and pick up what ingredients you don't have on the way home after work. Or you get hungry, find a recipe, get your groceries delivered, and start cooking within the hour. This book is for the spontaneous craving, which is how the chapters are separated. I encourage you to ask, "What do I want to eat?" instead of, "Have I eaten my recommended dose of legumes today?" Each chapter correlates to what you're craving. If you're looking for a little burn, head right to the Spicy & Hot chapter; if you want hot liquid to sit in your tummy, start at the Soupy & Slurpable chapter. If you're craving the vegan chapter, honey, this ain't that book.

Where to start? Here! No one except you will eat the food you make when you're living, cooking, and eating alone. There is freedom in that—you can cook whatever you want without opinions from the peanut gallery. I have a bland palate. I've been expanding said palate, but traditionally, I like *very* plain food, and the most seasoning I can handle is a lot of butter or cheese. I'm comin' around on cumin, but don't you dare come at me with paprika. Even cacio e pepe is spicy to me. I like plain cheese pizza, a hot dog with only ketchup, and a burger with only cheese and ketchup! Imagine the annoyance and frustration of having to factor in my dietary restrictions when you invite me over for dinner. Is this why I eat alone so often? I'll never know. But what I do know is that single servings are naturally difficult when it comes to figuring out spice and seasoning measurements. What makes this cookbook so unique is that we did the work and figured it out for you, so nothing tastes bland and everything is proportionally seasoned. There is no one way to cook for one, but here are some ideas to help guide you. They may also be helpful if you're cooking for two or for someone with varied taste buds, diets, eating schedules, or horoscopes. Good luck feeding your Scorpio friends!

Game Planning

You don't have to plan every meal ahead of time if you don't want to. You can let cravings guide your cooking.

Only purchase what you need, what brings you joy, and what will excite you. I often walk past the seafood aisle and see lobster tails on sale. Before this book, I would continue walking by—but with this book, giiiiiirl, I will stop and buy that fancy discounted seafood! (And eat it immediately! There's a reason it's on sale!)

When possible, buy ingredients you can use all at once, like a shallot instead of an onion or a sweet potato instead of a butternut squash. I can promise you right now there is no butternut squash in this book. It's too damned big.

Only purchase large quantities of multitasking ingredients. Think: *Do I know how to cook parsnips in more than two ways?* If yes, and you're excited by those prospects, go get 'em. If you are like me and do not know what a parsnip looks like, you shouldn't waste your time or money on large quantities of such make-believe things! I can promise you right now, there is no parsnip in this book. It's too damned made-up.

Hit the bulk bins so that you can purchase only the quantities that suit your needs. Here's looking at you, "single banana" section—or should I say, "Banana for One."

Leftovering

Avoid food waste and associated bad feelings. Ideally this book is helping you avoid leftovering, but sometimes shit happens. Some of these recipes will provide a little more than one serving, but look, I can't create half an egg, okay? Because even the best efforts go awry, know what to do with cooked meals that have seen brighter days. Great contenders are broth, soup, pasta sauce, frittatas, and tacos. Don't be eating this stuff, like, a week later. Remember, you are a luxury item. Perhaps it's a good time to look into composting. The best way to prevent waste is to cook only what you want to eat, and when you're cooking for one, that's easy to do. Lucky you!!!

Equipment

There are a handful of things I think your kitchen should have (ugh, is this the pantry staples I said I wouldn't provide??) because I used it, and I liked it. If you're going to do one big shopping run to prep, here's what I would buy that will be useful:

Timers: Your smartphone has one, but I have a couple magnetized ones that I put on my oven for ease when timing multiple things.

Immersion blender: This will come in handy in the soup chapter. I didn't know this existed and my life is better tenfold now that I own one. It's like the blender's cooler older sister who can drive stick.

6½ × 5-inch baking dish, 6-inch pie dish, and small baking sheets: Small servings are best made with small cookware.

Instant-read thermometer: Sure, you could guess, but why would you want to?

Geometry skills: It's helpful if you know what ½ inch looks like and the difference between a right triangle and an isosceles. No, seriously.

The will to live: Self-explanatory.

If, Then

I get annoyed at many things: people walking slowly, people coughing with their mouths open, people!! But specifically, I get annoyed when a recipe calls for an ingredient and then I use only a little of it and have so much left over. That is why this section exists. Here is a helpful guide to help you plan how to use some extra ingredients.

If you have a big jug of whole milk...

...then use some in the **Italian Divorce Soup** (page 30), **S'Mac Talk and Cheese** (page 84), **Chicken Potpie** (page 99), **Savory Dutch Baby, Baby** (page 104), **Banana Puddin'** (page 181), or **The Fellowship of the Lemon Ricotta Pancake** (page 196).

If you have extra scallion...

...then use them in **Send Noods, Chicken Soup Style** (page 25), **Not-Instant Ramen** (page 41), **Neato Frito Chili Pie** (page 44), **Rice Noodle Salad** (page 50), **Crispy Rice Spicy Tuna** (page 54), **Peanut Noodles** (page 58), **Ride or Die Pad Thai** (page 108), **Teriyaki Salmon** (page 131), **Spicy Pork Lettuce D-Cups** (page 159), **Double Dan the Noodles** (page 168), or **Pork and Chile Crisp Dumplings** (page 172).

If you have a giant piece of ginger...

...then use it in the **Not-Instant Ramen** (page 41), **Chicken Pho You** (page 38), **Peanut Noodles** (page 58), **Jollof Rice** (page 101), **Beef and Broccoli and You** (page 151), **Wind Beneath Your Orange-Ginger Chicken Wings** (page 140), **Spicy Pork Lettuce D-Cups** (page 159), or **Butter Tofu Just fo' You** (page 167).

If you have extra Italian sausage...

...then throw it in the **Italian Divorce Soup** (page 30), **Leave Me Alone Lasagna** (page 71), **Gnocchi with Sausage and Peppas** (page 92), or **Pork and Chile Crisp Dumplings** (page 172).

If you have ground pork...

...then use it in the **Not-Instant Ramen** (page 41), **This Little Piggy Became Pork Marbella Meatballs** (page 147), **Spicy Pork Lettuce D-Cups** (page 159), or **Double the Dan Noodles** (page 168).

If you have heavy cream...

...then use it in the **No-Hangover Vodka Pasta** (page 91), **Chicken Potpie** (page 99), **Under the Tuscan Chicken** (page 152), **Butter Tofu Just fo' You** (page 167), **Strawberry Shawtycake** (page 177), or **Banana Puddin'** (page 181).

If you have extra chicken thighs...

...then use them in **Send Noods, Chicken Soup Style** (page 25), **Chicken Potpie** (page 99), **Chicken Shawarma** (page 120), or **BBQ Pulled Chicken Sandwich** (page 143).

If you have extra chicken breasts...

...then use them in the **Chicken Parm Nuggets** (page 79), **She's Piccata Have It (Chicken)** (page 144), **Under the Tuscan Chicken** (page 152), or **How Now Brown Kung Pao Chicken** (page 164).

If you have white wine...

...then damn, you didn't just finish the bottle? Okay, you can use it in the **Salty French One-Yon Soup** (page 33), **Rizzo-tto with Peas and Parm** (page 96), **You Say Potato, I Say Galette** (page 107), **She's Piccata Have It (Chicken)** (page 144), or **This Little Piggy Became Pork Marbella Meatballs** (page 147).

If you have a big ol' loaf of sourdough...

...then serve those slices with **Tomato Soup with Grilled Cheese Croutons** (page 26), **Salty French One-Yon Soup** (page 33), **Caprese Salad with Crispy Prosciutto** (page 61), or **Hail (Kale) Caesar** (page 53).

If you are still reading this...

...then you are ready to start cooking!

Soupy &

Slurpable

Send Noods, Chicken Soup Style

We're starting the book off with a BANG, which is usually what one hopes for when you send tasteful *nudes*. While tasteful, these *noods* are noodles in a savory, delicious chicken soup. Perfect for yourself or delivering to that special someone you hope to see naked.

Serves 1

1 tablespoon unsalted butter

½ small yellow onion, or 1 medium shallot, finely chopped (about ½ cup)

2 teaspoons chicken bouillon paste (or use 2¼ cups chicken broth and skip the water)

1 (5- to 6-ounce) boneless, skinless chicken thigh, or heaping ½ cup shredded rotisserie chicken

¼ teaspoon freshly ground black pepper

½ cup (or up to 1 cup if you love them) wide egg noodles (see Note)

1 small carrot, thinly sliced (about ⅓ cup)

1 small celery stalk, thinly sliced (about ¼ cup)

1 lemon wedge (optional, but highly recommended)

1 tablespoon coarsely chopped celery leaves, for garnish

1 tablespoon coarsely chopped fresh herbs like parsley, dill, or scallion, for garnish (optional, only if you have them)

1. Melt the butter in a small pot over medium heat. When the butter is foaming, add the onion and cook, stirring almost continuously to prevent browning, until soft and translucent, about 2 minutes. Add 2¼ cups water and bring to a boil. Stir in the bouillon paste until it dissolves.

2. If you're using rotisserie chicken, skip to the next step. If you're cooking raw chicken: Add the chicken to the pot, reduce the heat to medium-low so the water bubbles very gently, and cover the pot. Cook until the chicken is cooked through (you can check by cutting into it with a paring knife—if it's not pink, you're good), 10 to 15 minutes. Remove the chicken from the broth and let it rest for 5 minutes, then use two forks to shred it.

3. Increase the heat to medium and return the broth to a boil. Add the pepper, then add the egg noodles and cook according to the package directions until al dente. Three minutes before the noodles are ready, add the shredded chicken, the carrot, and the celery to warm them through. When the noodles are done, squeeze a few drops of lemon juice into the soup to brighten it up, if desired.

4. Ladle your soup into a bowl, then sprinkle the celery leaves and herbs (if using) over the top and eat right away.

Tomato Soup with Grilled Cheese Croutons

Up until this recipe, I wasn't much of a tomato soup gal, but then . . . this recipe made its way into my heart and mouth. I love grilled cheese with soup, but I simply cannot handle that much dairy, so a compromise was made by adding crispy cheese-topped croutons. Bisque-like and perfect for a winter meal, this soup will leave your kitchen smelling great even after it's gone, which should be the same day because, well, single servings.

Serves 1

2 medium plum tomatoes (8 to 10 ounces total), quartered lengthwise

1 tablespoon extra-virgin olive oil

¼ teaspoon kosher salt

¼ teaspoon freshly ground black pepper

1 slice sourdough or other good crusty bread, cubed

½ cup shredded sharp cheddar cheese

1 tablespoon unsalted butter

½ small yellow onion, or 1 medium shallot, finely chopped (about ½ cup)

1 garlic clove, finely chopped

⅛ teaspoon red pepper flakes (optional)

1 heaping teaspoon tomato paste

1 teaspoon chicken bouillon paste (or use 1 cup chicken broth or vegetable broth and skip the water)

1 teaspoon sugar

¼ teaspoon dried thyme

1 tablespoon heavy cream, or 2 tablespoons half-and-half

1. Preheat the oven to 400°F. Line a baking sheet with parchment paper or aluminum foil.

2. Place the tomatoes on one side of the prepared baking sheet and toss with half the olive oil and the salt and pepper. Arrange them cut-side down and bake for 5 minutes. Remove the pan from the oven, add the bread cubes to the other side, and drizzle with the remaining olive oil. Bake for 12 minutes, until the bread is mostly browned and crisped. Remove from the oven and sprinkle the cheese evenly over the bread. (Getting some cheese on the pan is good—that means crispy bits!) Bake for about 5 minutes more, until the tomatoes start to release some juices and get a little color on the edges and the cheese is melted, bubbling, and crispy on the edges.

3. Meanwhile, in a small pot, melt the butter over medium heat. When the butter is foaming, add the onion and cook, stirring almost continuously to prevent browning, until soft and translucent, about 5 minutes. Add the garlic and red pepper flakes (if using) and cook, stirring often until fragrant, about 1 minute. Add the tomato paste and cook, stirring continuously, until it darkens a few shades but before it starts to stick to the bottom of the pot, 1 to 2 minutes.

4. Pour in 1 cup water, then add the bouillon paste, sugar, and thyme. Stir, scraping up all the browned bits from the bottom of the pan, and bring to a simmer. Reduce the heat to low, cover, and simmer for 10 minutes.

5. Carefully add the roasted tomatoes to the pot, along with any juices and caramelized bits on the baking sheet. Increase the heat to medium and return the soup to a simmer. Cook for 10 minutes more, just to let the flavors combine. Remove from the heat and use an immersion blender to puree the soup directly in the pot. (If you don't have one, ladle the soup into a standing blender but only fill it up halfway—work in batches if your blender is small. Crack the lid away from you to allow steam to escape and protect your hand with a kitchen towel, then blend until the soup is smooth and return it to the pot.)

6. Pour the cream into the soup and stir. Break apart the croutons and sprinkle them and the crispy bits of cheese on top of the soup. Serve right away.

Highland Park Matzo Ball Soup

I grew up in a suburb outside Chicago called Highland Park that boasts a vibrant Jewish community, and one of the delis in town was famous for their matzo ball soup. That's how I got introduced to it and it was love at first dill. When I went to college and subsequently left Illinois, I longed for the deli soup and had to replace it with the boxed Manischewitz Matzo Ball & Soup version, but boxed soup no more. This is a favorite both when I'm homesick and when I'm home, sick.

Serves 1

Matzo Ball Mix

1 large egg

1 tablespoon vegetable oil, such as canola

1 teaspoon finely chopped fresh dill

½ teaspoon kosher salt

⅛ teaspoon onion powder

⅛ teaspoon garlic powder

¼ cup matzo meal

1 tablespoon seltzer water or club soda

Soup

2 teaspoons chicken bouillon paste (or use 3 cups chicken broth and skip the water)

Pinch of freshly ground black pepper

1 small carrot, thinly sliced

Kosher salt (optional)

1 tablespoon finely chopped fresh dill, for garnish

1. **Make the matzo ball mix:** In a small bowl, whisk together the egg and oil with a fork until no streaks of egg white remain. Add the dill, salt, onion powder, and garlic powder and whisk until thoroughly incorporated. Stir in the matzo meal and seltzer until evenly mixed. Cover the bowl with plastic wrap or a lid and refrigerate for at least 3 hours or up to overnight.

2. **Make the soup:** In a medium saucepan, bring 3 cups water to a boil over medium-high heat. Add the bouillon paste and pepper and stir until the paste has dissolved.

3. Wet your hands and portion the matzo ball mix into three equal pieces. Roll each piece in your hands to form a smooth, even ball, then gently drop it into the boiling broth. Reduce the heat to medium-low so the soup simmers steadily, cover, and cook for 15 minutes. Peek after 15 minutes—if the matzo balls are floating, they're probably ready (the real test is to sacrifice one matzo ball by cutting it in half to make sure it's the same light color and texture throughout, but since we only have three, we'll give them a nice long simmer instead). If they're not floating yet, cover and cook for 5 minutes more, then check again.

4. Add the carrot to the soup, cover, and simmer just until the carrot is a little tender, about 5 minutes, then remove from the heat. (If you used broth, taste and see if the soup needs salt at this point. If you used bouillon, it shouldn't.)

5. Transfer the matzo balls and carrots to a bowl, ladle over as much of the broth as you like (there's a lot!), sprinkle with the dill, and serve.

Italian Divorce Soup

This is your typical wedding soup but better because while weddings can be nice, so can a divorce! I've had neither, but a friend who recently got divorced told me that she hated telling people she had gotten divorced because they'd get a sad look on their face and say, "I'm sorry." This soup is for the newly single who instead want you to say, "CONGRATULATIONS!!!" Unlike the broth and meatballs you're about to make, not everything is a good match and that's perfectly okay. Substitute that absent wedding ring for extra ditalini (they look like rings).

Serves 1

- 2 tablespoons panko breadcrumbs
- 1 tablespoon whole milk or water
- 1 sweet Italian sausage, casing removed
- 4 tablespoons freshly and finely grated Parmigiano Reggiano cheese
- ⅛ teaspoon kosher salt
- ⅛ teaspoon dried oregano or Italian seasoning
- 1 tablespoon extra-virgin olive oil
- ½ small yellow onion, or 1 medium shallot, finely chopped (about ½ cup)
- 1 garlic clove, chopped
- 2 teaspoons chicken bouillon paste (or use 2 cups chicken broth and skip the water)
- ⅛ teaspoon freshly ground black pepper
- ¼ cup ditalini or other tiny pasta
- 2 cups loosely packed finely chopped escarole, kale, or baby spinach
- 1 heaping tablespoon finely chopped fresh flat-leaf parsley, for garnish

1. In a small bowl, mix the breadcrumbs and milk and let stand until the breadcrumbs have absorbed the liquid, 2 to 3 minutes. Add the sausage, 2 tablespoons of the Parmesan, the salt, and the oregano. Mix everything with clean hands just until thoroughly and evenly combined, then stop mixing, or the meatballs will be tough.

2. Divide the mixture into 8 small balls. Return them to the bowl and refrigerate, uncovered, for 10 minutes while you make the broth.

3. Heat the olive oil in a small pot over medium heat for 1 minute. Add a piece of onion to the pot—if it sizzles immediately, the oil is hot enough; if not, wait a minute and try again. Add all the onion and cook, stirring almost continuously to prevent browning, until softened and translucent, 2 to 3 minutes. Add the garlic and cook, stirring often, until fragrant, about 30 seconds. Pour in 2 cups water, then add the bouillon paste and stir until it has dissolved. Season with the pepper and bring to a simmer.

4. Add the pasta and cook according to the package directions until al dente. When the pasta has 6 minutes left, add the meatballs and escarole and stir gently to combine. Cook until the greens are wilted, the meatballs are cooked through, and the pasta is al dente. Remove from the heat.

5. Stir in the parsley, then ladle the soup into a bowl. Garnish with the remaining 2 tablespoons Parmesan and serve right away.

Salty French One-Yon Soup

Bonjour, oui oui, wassup, it's salty soup time. The French are good at many things: speaking French, building cool structures, using cheese . . . just to name a few. This is perfect for the days you're feeling international but are salty that you aren't traveling! A classic French dish, this soup is caramelized onions mixed with a beefy wine broth underneath the most delicious piece of toasty cheese bread you've ever had, and it's perfect for one(yon). My non-meat-eating friends aren't getting left behind, either, as there's a vegetarian version.

Serves 1

- 1 tablespoon unsalted butter
- 1 pound yellow or red onions (1 very large or 2 medium), sliced
- ½ teaspoon kosher salt
- ¼ teaspoon freshly ground black pepper
- ¼ cup white wine
- 2 teaspoons beef bouillon paste (or use 2 cups beef bone broth and skip the water)
- 1 bay leaf, or 1 sprig thyme
- 1 thick slice sourdough or other good crusty bread
- ¼ cup packed freshly grated Gruyère cheese (1 ounce)

1. Melt the butter in a medium skillet over medium-high heat. Add the onions, season with the salt and pepper, cover and cook, stirring only once or twice, until the onions are softened and starting to brown in spots, 7 to 10 minutes. Uncover, reduce the heat to medium-low, and cook, stirring occasionally, until deep golden brown, 20 to 25 minutes. Every 5 minutes or so, or if the onions threaten to burn, add a few tablespoons of water, scraping up any browned bits that are stuck to the bottom of the skillet.
2. Add the wine, increase the heat to medium-high, and simmer until syrupy, 2 to 3 minutes. Add 2 cups water, the bouillon paste, and the bay leaf and stir to dissolve the bouillon. Bring to a simmer, then reduce the heat to medium-low. Simmer, scraping up all the browned bits from the bottom of the pan, until flavorful and slightly thickened, 10 to 15 minutes.
3. Meanwhile, position a rack in the upper third of the oven and preheat the broiler to high.
4. Broil the bread until toasted on one side, 1 to 2 minutes.
5. Remove the bay leaf from the soup. Pour the soup into a small ovenproof bowl or baking dish that holds at least 2 cups (your trusty 6½ × 5-inch pan will work) and put that on a small baking sheet. Place the bread toasted-side down into the soup (cut it to fit, if needed). Sprinkle with the cheese, then broil until the cheese is bubbling and golden, 1 to 2 minutes. Dig in.

Vegetarian French Onion Soup: Omit the beef bouillon paste and add 1 tablespoon heavy cream with the water and bay leaf. Once the soup has thickened and the flavors have come together, stir in 2 teaspoons soy sauce and 1 teaspoon balsamic vinegar. Taste it, and if you love vinegar, add another teaspoon.

Beef and Barley Soup

Short rib? In a soup? You bet your barley, baby. When I tested this recipe, I almost ran out of beef because I couldn't stop nibbling while making the broth. This is a heartier soup that will leave you a little fuller than the others, so bring out the sweatpants. Unless you're like me and are already wearing them.

Serves 1 generously

8 ounces boneless short rib, cut into ½-inch cubes

½ teaspoon kosher salt

½ teaspoon freshly ground black pepper

1 tablespoon vegetable oil, such as canola

1 small carrot, diced (about ¼ cup)

1 small celery stalk, diced (about ¼ cup)

½ small yellow onion, or 1 medium shallot, diced (about ½ cup)

1 garlic clove, minced

1 teaspoon tomato paste

2 teaspoons chicken bouillon paste or beef bouillon paste (or use 2 cups stock and skip the water)

½ teaspoon dried thyme

1 bay leaf

¼ cup pearled barley

1 tablespoon fresh flat-leaf parsley, for garnish

1. Season the meat all over with the salt and ¼ teaspoon of the pepper. Heat the oil in a Dutch oven or heavy-bottomed medium pot over medium-high heat for a couple of minutes. Add the meat to the pot and spread it into a single layer. Cook until the juices cook off and the meat is sizzling and well browned on the bottom, about 7 minutes, then cook, stirring just a few times, until the meat is browned on two sides, about 3 minutes more. Transfer the meat to a plate.

2. Reduce the heat to medium-low. Add the carrot, celery, onion, and garlic to the pot and cook, stirring continuously, for a minute or so, just to scrape up any browned bits from the bottom of the pot. Add the tomato paste and cook, stirring continuously, for 30 seconds, just until you can smell it. Pour in 2 cups water, add the bouillon paste, thyme, bay leaf, and remaining ¼ teaspoon pepper, and stir.

3. Return the meat to the pot, along with any juices that have accumulated on the plate, and bring the soup to a simmer. Reduce the heat to low so the soup bubbles gently, cover, and simmer until the beef is starting to get tender, about 1 hour.

4. Add the barley, cover, and cook, stirring and checking on the water level occasionally (add more water if it starts to get low), until the meat and barley are tender, about 45 minutes. Ladle into a bowl, sprinkle with the parsley, and serve!

Gentle Lentil Soup

Time to whip out that immersion blender! Despite the title, you're about to rock those lentils' world with this slurpable, flavorful soup. Don't make around friends, because there isn't enough to share, and I doubt they'll be gentle when they try to wrestle the bowl away from you.

Serves 1

1 tablespoon extra-virgin olive oil

1 small carrot, finely chopped (¼ to ⅓ cup)

1 medium shallot, or ½ small yellow onion, finely chopped (about ½ cup)

1 small celery stalk, finely chopped (about ¼ cup)

1 garlic clove, minced

1 heaping teaspoon tomato paste

1 teaspoon chili powder

¼ cup dried red lentils, rinsed

1 heaping teaspoon chicken bouillon paste (see Note)

⅛ teaspoon freshly ground black pepper

For Serving

¼ cup crumbled feta cheese, plain full-fat Greek yogurt, or full-fat sour cream

¼ cup cilantro sprigs

½ lime

1. Heat the olive oil in a small pot over medium heat for 1 minute. Add a piece of carrot—if it sizzles immediately, the oil is hot enough; if not, wait a minute and try again. Add the carrot, shallot, and celery and cook, stirring almost continuously to prevent browning, until the shallot is soft and translucent and the other vegetables are beginning to soften, about 5 minutes. Add the garlic and cook, stirring continuously, until fragrant, about 30 seconds. Stir in the tomato paste and chili powder and cook, stirring continuously, until the paste darkens and caramelizes (but don't let it scorch!), 1 to 2 minutes.

2. Add 1¼ cups water, the lentils, bouillon paste, and pepper and stir to combine. Bring to a simmer, then reduce the heat to medium-low so the soup bubbles gently and cover, leaving the lid cracked. Cook, stirring every so often to make sure nothing is sticking to the bottom, until the lentils and vegetables are tender, about 25 minutes. Remove from the heat, then, using an immersion blender, pulse a few times to thicken the soup. (If you don't have an immersion blender, mash some of the lentils against the side of the pot with a spoon.) If the soup is too thick for your taste, stir in water 1 tablespoon at a time until you achieve your desired consistency.

3. Transfer the soup to a bowl, top with the feta and cilantro, and (this is the key part) squeeze the lime juice into your bowl, then serve!

Note

To make the soup vegetarian, use a vegetable bouillon paste, or skip the bouillon and water and use 1¼ cups vegetable broth and ½ teaspoon kosher salt instead.

Chicken Pho You

Trying new food (aka food with flavor, seasoning, or spice) used to scare me, so I lived a deprived life without pho until I was twenty-four. I had gotten an assistant job to a TV producer, and our office was in Hollywood. I knew immediately it was going to be a great job because when the bosses ordered in lunch, the assistants got it, too. When you're twenty-four, poor, and desperately trying to make your dreams come true, free lunch is a game changer. One of the regular spots we went to was a pho restaurant, and after so many fried rice lunches, my coworker Charles convinced me to try pho, and I've never looked back. A traditional Vietnamese soup, pho, pronounced *fuh*, will make you feel like a Glam Hollywood Assistant, aka you will make more broth than you need for one, but you can freeze and reuse it to help that cobwebbed wallet. The recipe calls for rotisserie chicken, but see the variation if you want to sub in chicken thighs.

Makes enough broth for 4 servings

- 1 (3-pound) rotisserie chicken
- 1 large yellow onion, unpeeled, root end trimmed
- 1 large jalapeño
- 1 small bunch cilantro
- 1 teaspoon whole black peppercorns
- 1 teaspoon coriander seeds
- 4 whole cloves
- 1 (4-inch) piece fresh ginger, unpeeled, halved lengthwise
- 2 tablespoons fish sauce
- 1 tablespoon chicken bouillon paste
- 2 teaspoons rock sugar or granulated sugar

For Serving

- 4 ounces thin, flat rice noodles
- ½ lime, cut into wedges
- Hoisin and/or sriracha or other condiments of your choice (optional)

1. Remove all the meat from the chicken, reserving the bones, skin, and any juices from the container. Shred the meat, pop it in an airtight container, and refrigerate until ready to serve.

2. Use a very sharp knife to cut the onion in half (it doesn't matter which way), then cut off about a 1-inch piece from one half and peel just that small bit. Cut the peeled piece into very thin slices; set those aside for serving. Halve the jalapeño crosswise and cut as many very thin slices as you want for your soup; set them aside for serving. Remove enough cilantro leaves and tender stems to make ½ loosely packed cup and set that aside for serving. Now your toppings are ready to go!

3. In a large Dutch oven or other heavy-bottomed pot, combine the peppercorns, coriander seeds, and cloves and toast over medium heat, stirring often, until fragrant, 2 to 3 minutes. Transfer the spices to a plate. Increase the heat to medium-high and place the unpeeled onion halves, the unsliced jalapeño, and the ginger to the pot cut-side down and cook, turning only as each side chars, until charred all over, 8 to 10 minutes total.

4. Add the reserved chicken bones, skin, and juices to the pot and pour in 12 cups water. Bring to a boil over high heat. Use a large spoon to skim off and discard any foam and fat that rise to the top. (This keeps the broth clear, which is what we want!) When the broth is boiling and you've removed most of the foam at the top, add the remaining cilantro, the fish sauce, bouillon paste, and sugar

Recipe continues

and return the toasted spices to the pot. Return the broth to a boil, then reduce the heat to medium or medium-low so the soup simmers gently and cook, occasionally skimming any foam from the surface, until the broth is flavorful and fragrant, 30 to 45 minutes.

5. When the broth is done, strain it through a fine-mesh strainer set over a large bowl or another pot; discard the solids. Set aside 2 cups of broth for serving; let the rest cool until warm, divide it into 2-cup airtight containers, and freeze for up to 3 months. (Pro tip: You can also divide the shredded chicken among the broth portions and freeze them together.)

6. When you're getting close to serving time, put the rice noodles in a medium bowl and add warm water to cover. Soak for 30 minutes (this helps them cook more quickly and evenly), then drain.

7. Bring a small saucepan of water to a boil over high heat. Add the noodles and cook until tender; this should take just a couple of minutes, since they were soaked, but the total time will depend on the type of noodles—start checking after 2 minutes. Drain and quickly rinse the noodles, then transfer to a large serving bowl.

8. In the same saucepan, combine the reserved 2 cups broth and as much chicken as you like (save the rest for other meals, if you didn't freeze it with the extra broth). Bring to a simmer over medium heat. Pour the hot broth and chicken over the noodles and add the reserved sliced onion, sliced jalapeño, and cilantro. Serve with the lime wedges on the side and any condiments of your choice.

Rotisserie-Free Stock: Omit the rotisserie chicken from the first step, but do all the same prep for the aromatics. Skip the bouillon paste and use 1 pound boneless, skinless chicken thighs and 3 quarts chicken bone broth instead. In the third step, add the chicken thighs and bone broth to the pot, and skim any foam on the top as it comes to a boil. After 20 minutes of simmering, check to see if the chicken is cooked through (no pink inside at all). If it is, remove it from the pot and set it aside to cool for 5 minutes, then shred the meat with two forks. If it's not, simmer for 5 minutes more, then check again. Finish and strain the broth as directed, and divide the shredded chicken among the portions of broth you're going to freeze.

Not-Instant Ramen

When I was younger and had the organs of a Greek god, shrimp-flavor instant cup noodles was a delicious remedy when I was sick, and up until my early thirties, that's what I thought ramen was. Hahahaha, no. After a trip to Japan, where I tasted real ramen, I realized my grave error. I'm partial to tonkotsu, which has a broth made from pork bones, and wanted to include it in this book. Then I saw how much work went into it and was like, nah, fam, we ain't be doing all that. This is a step up from instant ramen because the pork and aromatics give it a nice, rich flavor, though not like a true garlicky tonkotsu broth because it certainly doesn't require twelve hours to cook. You ain't got time for that.

Serves 1

1 large egg, in the shell

1 (5- to 6-ounce) package fresh ramen noodles or 3 ounces dried (not instant) ramen noodles

1 head baby bok choy, quartered lengthwise

1 teaspoon vegetable oil, such as canola

4 ounces ground pork

½ medium shallot, or ¼ small yellow onion, finely chopped

1 (½-inch) piece fresh ginger, peeled and grated

2 garlic cloves, grated

1 heaping teaspoon chicken bouillon paste (or use 2 cups chicken broth and skip the water)

1 teaspoon soy sauce

1 teaspoon mirin, or ½ teaspoon sugar

¼ teaspoon instant dashi powder

Kosher salt (optional)

¼ cup frozen corn kernels, thawed

2 scallions, thinly sliced, or 4 fresh chives, chopped

¼ nori sheet (or a seaweed snack, if that's all you have)

Chive Blossoms, for topping (optional)

1. Fill a small pot with 3 inches of water and bring to a boil over high heat. Fill a small bowl with cold water and a handful of ice.

2. Gently lower the whole egg into the boiling water. As soon as the egg is in the water, reduce the heat to medium so it simmers vigorously but isn't at a rapid boil and set a timer for 6½ minutes for a runny egg or 7½ minutes for a jammy egg. When the timer goes off, use a spoon or tongs to transfer the egg to the ice bath, leaving the water in the pot (we are saving pots, energy, and water here). Let the egg cool in the water for 5 minutes, then remove it; reserve the ice water.

3. Meanwhile, return the saucepan of water to a boil (top it off, if necessary). Add the noodles and cook according to the package directions. Remove the noodles with tongs or a slotted spoon and shake off any excess water, then place them in a large serving bowl.

4. Bring the water back to a boil one last time, add the bok choy, and cook until bright green and the stems are starting to get tender, about 2 minutes. Drain, transfer to the bowl of ice water to cool for 2 minutes, and drain again.

5. Heat the oil in a medium saucepan over medium heat for 1 minute. Add the ground pork and immediately start breaking it up with your spoon into very small pieces. Cook, breaking up the meat and stirring continuously, until there is no visible pink, about 1 minute. Add the shallot and cook, stirring regularly, until the meat is cooked through and the shallot is translucent, 2 to 3 minutes more. Add the ginger and garlic and cook until fragrant, about 30 seconds.

Recipe continues

6. Pour 2 cups water into the pot and bring to a boil, then immediately remove the pot from the heat. Stir in the bouillon paste, soy sauce, mirin, and dashi powder until the paste is broken up. Taste and add a pinch of salt, if it needs it (it might not, depending on your bouillon).

7. Pour the broth into the serving bowl with the noodles and top with the bok choy, corn, and scallions. Peel the egg, halve it lengthwise, and add it to the bowl. Tuck the nori sheet into the side and eat.

Vegetarian Ramen: Replace the ground pork with 3 fresh shiitake mushrooms, stemmed and sliced. Cook them in 1 tablespoon oil until they're beginning to brown, about 3 minutes, then add the shallot and cook until the shallot is translucent, 2 to 3 minutes more. Add the ginger and garlic and cook as directed. Use vegetable bouillon paste and water, or vegetable stock, and replace the dashi powder with 1 teaspoon white miso paste.

Neato Frito Chili Pie

Of course chili on its own is good, but for colder weather, topping it with some corn chips makes it even better. While it's not a pie in the traditional sense, the layered structure and scoop-ability from the dish is what gives it pie vibes. This will be enough for lunch and dinner, or if you've just moved into your own place, a gift for your new neighbor.

Serves 2

8 ounces ground beef (ideally a fatty blend like 80/20)

½ small white onion, finely chopped

½ teaspoon kosher salt

3 garlic cloves, minced

1 tablespoon tomato paste

2 teaspoons taco seasoning (or chili powder, if that's what you've got)

½ teaspoon dried oregano

1 (15-ounce) can pinto, black, or kidney beans, drained and rinsed

1 (15-ounce) can diced tomatoes (if you like a chunky chili), or 1 (15-ounce) can pureed tomatoes (if you like it smoother)

1 (12-ounce) can beer, like a lager (optional)

1 teaspoon light brown sugar

1 teaspoon apple cider vinegar

1 teaspoon soy sauce

For Serving

1 (3.5-ounce) bag Fritos

½ small white onion, diced

½ cup shredded cheddar cheese

Optional toppings (choose as many as you like): pickled jalapeño slices, diced avocado, cilantro sprigs, sliced scallions, sour cream

1. Heat a medium or large heavy-bottomed pot over medium-high heat for a few minutes. Add the beef and spread it into an even layer, then cook, undisturbed, for 5 minutes. Break up the beef with a spoon and cook until it is crumbled, browned, and crisp, 1 to 2 minutes more (you don't have to worry about cooking it all the way through yet). Tilt the pan slightly and use the spoon to transfer the beef to a plate, leaving the fat in the pot.

2. Reduce the heat to medium-low, then add the onion and ¼ teaspoon of the salt. Cook, stirring often and scraping up any browned bits from the bottom of the pot, until the onion is soft and browned on the edges, about 3 minutes. Add the garlic and cook, stirring continuously, until fragrant, 30 seconds. Add the tomato paste, taco seasoning, and oregano and cook, stirring continuously, until the paste and spices are evenly distributed among the onions, sizzling, and fragrant, 1 to 2 minutes.

3. Pour in the beans, tomatoes, 1 cup of the beer (if using; save the rest for drinking), the brown sugar, and the remaining ¼ teaspoon salt. Return the beef to the pot, along with any juices accumulated on the plate. Stir to combine, then bring to a boil. Reduce the heat to medium-low to maintain a gentle simmer and cook, uncovered, stirring a few times, until it is thick and the flavors have melded, 30 to 40 minutes. Stir in the vinegar and soy sauce. Taste the chili; depending on how much salt is in the taco seasoning you used, you may need to add more.

4. Divide the Fritos between two bowls. Ladle the chili on top, sprinkle with the onion and cheese, and add as many more toppings as you like/have on hand/can handle. Let the cheese melt for a minute or two, then eat your Frito pie with a fork. The leftover bowl can be covered or transferred to an airtight container and stored in the refrigerator for 3 to 4 days; reheat it in the microwave.

Plain Old Chili: Skip the Fritos (or buy one of those tiny 1-ounce bags and crush them over the top) and serve the chili with as many toppings as you like. (Eat it with a spoon!)

Chill &

Salady

Halloumi Fattoush

Along the continued theme of my food ignorance, I was first introduced to Halloumi by my friend Natalie when she used to live in Williamsburg, or, as the young and sexy call it, WillyB*. She took me to an Israeli café nearby and shoved a slice of Halloumi in my mouth. That salty, squeaky cheese was life-changing—I saw stars. Which might've been because I briefly choked on it, but who is to say. Fattoush is a salad with Mediterranean roots that's fresh but filling, and the pita adds a nice crunch.

***No one calls it that.**

Serves 1

Dressing

1 tablespoon extra-virgin olive oil

1 tablespoon fresh lemon juice (from about ½ lemon)

1 tablespoon pomegranate molasses

1 garlic clove, grated

1 teaspoon ground sumac

1 teaspoon kosher salt

Pinch of freshly ground black pepper

Salad

1 small ripe tomato, cut into bite-size pieces

2 tablespoons extra-virgin olive oil, plus more as needed

1 pita, torn into bite-size pieces

Pinch of kosher salt

½ (8-ounce or so) package Halloumi cheese, cut into bite-size cubes

1 small head romaine lettuce, leaves separated and cut into bite-size pieces

1 Persian (mini) cucumber, cut into bite-size pieces

¼ small red onion, thinly sliced

3 radishes, trimmed and thinly sliced

¼ cup fresh mint leaves

1 teaspoon pomegranate molasses, for serving

1. **Make the dressing:** In a small jar or bowl, combine the olive oil, lemon juice, molasses, garlic, sumac, salt, and pepper. Cover the jar and shake until emulsified or whisk until smooth.

2. **Make the salad:** Place the tomato in a colander and set it in the sink to drain excess liquid.

3. Line a plate with a paper towel. Heat the olive oil in a medium nonstick skillet over medium heat for a couple of minutes. Add a piece of pita to the pan—if it sizzles immediately, the oil is hot enough; if not, wait until it's sizzling to add the rest of the pita. Cook the pita, stirring often, until the pita is golden and crisp all over, 3 to 5 minutes. Transfer the pita to the paper towel–lined plate, leaving any remaining oil in the pan. Season the pita with the salt.

4. Place the Halloumi in the pan and cook, shaking the pan every 30 seconds or so, until the cubes are golden on most sides (you don't have to get every single side), 2 to 3 minutes total. Transfer the Halloumi to the paper towel with the pita.

5. In a large bowl, combine the lettuce, cucumber, onion, radishes, mint, drained tomato, and Halloumi. Shake or stir the dressing, then drizzle the salad with about half the dressing and toss. Taste the salad and see if it needs more dressing (store any extra in the fridge for up to 3 days). Right before serving, add the fried pita and toss again. Drizzle with the molasses, sprinkle with the sumac, and eat.

Rice Noodle Salad

Yeah, see, if you just add "salad" at the end, that makes it so. This *salad* is very green and leans more toward a Thai-style dish due to its use of flat noodles instead of vermicelli, which is more for a Vietnamese-style salad. Tofu adds protein, but feel free to swap it with a protein of your choosing. It's a great "salad" for a hotter day to keep your mouth cool.

Serves 1

Dressing

1 tablespoon fish sauce (or plant-based fish sauce to make it vegan)

1 tablespoon fresh lime juice (from about 1 lime)

1 tablespoon distilled white vinegar

2 teaspoons sugar

¼ teaspoon kosher salt

1 garlic clove, minced or grated

Salad

4 ounces flat rice noodles

4 ounces extra-firm tofu

2¼ teaspoons kosher salt

1 tablespoon vegetable oil, such as canola

½ cup frozen edamame

2 romaine lettuce leaves, thinly sliced crosswise

2 scallions, thinly sliced on the diagonal

Handful of snap peas, trimmed and thinly sliced on the diagonal

¼ cup cilantro sprigs, coarsely chopped

8 fresh mint leaves, thinly sliced

½ small fresh green chile, such as serrano, or 1 small jalapeño, or to taste, halved, seeded, and sliced

¼ cup store-bought crispy fried shallots or onions, for serving

1. **Make the dressing:** In a medium bowl, whisk together 2 tablespoons water, the fish sauce, lime juice, vinegar, sugar, salt, and garlic until the sugar is dissolved.

2. **Make the salad:** Place the rice noodles in a medium bowl and cover with warm water. Soak for 30 minutes, then drain.

3. Pat the tofu dry with a paper towel and keep it wrapped in the same towel. Place a heavy item, like a cast-iron skillet, plate, or book, on top for 5 to 10 minutes to release excess liquid. Remove the towel, cut it into roughly ½-inch cubes, and season with ¼ teaspoon of the salt.

4. Heat the oil in a small nonstick skillet over medium-high heat for a couple of minutes. Add a piece of tofu to the pan—if it sizzles immediately, the oil is hot enough; if not, wait until it's sizzling before adding the rest of the tofu. Cook, stirring every couple of minutes, until the tofu is golden and crisp on two or three sides, about 5 minutes total. Transfer the tofu to the bowl with the dressing and let it marinate while you prepare the other ingredients.

5. Bring a small pot of water to a boil over high heat. Add the remaining 2 teaspoons salt and the noodles and cook until they are tender; the total time will depend on the type of noodle, but start checking after 2 minutes. Just before the noodles are done, add the edamame to the pot to warm through. Drain the noodles and edamame and rinse with cool water to stop the cooking.

6. In a serving bowl, combine the drained noodles and edamame, the lettuce, scallions, snap peas, cilantro, mint, chile, and tofu. Drizzle about half the dressing over the salad and toss, making sure everything is well coated. Taste and add more dressing if you think it needs it. Sprinkle with the crispy shallots and serve.

Hail (Kale) Caesar

Before you become a big fancy somebody, you first have to be a small unfancy assistant to a big fancy somebody, which is what I did for several years. Of the many things I learned from assisting other people, knowing where to get a good salad is a prized skill. I am a person of simple tastes, so you know I'm a lil' freak for a Caesar salad. My favorite one hails from Sweetgreen and inspired this Caesar's kale base. Even though the salad's name has nothing to do with Julius Caesar, I dedicate this salad to him. RIP, my dude. Maybe if you'd stayed home that fifteenth of March and made a single-serving salad, you wouldn't have been stabbed by your bros.

Serves 1

Salad

1 cup cubed nice crusty bread (½-inch cubes)

1 tablespoon extra-virgin olive oil

½ teaspoon kosher salt

6 tablespoons freshly and finely grated Parmigiano Reggiano cheese

2 chicken breast tenders (about 4 ounces total)

¼ teaspoon freshly ground black pepper

1 cup finely chopped stemmed curly kale leaves

1 cup finely chopped romaine lettuce

Dressing

1 to 2 anchovy fillet

1 tablespoon fresh lemon juice

½ teaspoon Dijon mustard

¼ teaspoon Worcestershire sauce

1 garlic clove, grated

Big pinch of freshly ground black pepper

2 tablespoons mayonnaise

1 tablespoon freshly and finely grated Parmigiano Reggiano cheese

1 tablespoon extra-virgin olive oil

For Serving

1 tablespoon freshly and finely grated Parmigiano Reggiano cheese

1 lemon wedge

1. **Make the salad:** Preheat the oven to 425°F. Line a baking sheet with parchment paper or aluminum foil.

2. Spread the bread cubes over one side of the baking sheet, drizzle with about half the olive oil, and season with ¼ teaspoon of the salt. Toss to coat, then sprinkle 4 tablespoons of the Parmesan over the bread, but do not stir. Place the chicken on the other side of the baking sheet and drizzle with the remaining olive oil, making sure it's coated all over. Season the chicken with the remaining ¼ teaspoon salt and the pepper.

3. Bake for about 10 minutes, until the chicken reads 165°F on an instant-read thermometer or is opaque all the way through and the croutons are browned with lots of crispy bits of cheese. Remove from the oven and let cool for 5 minutes.

4. Place the kale and romaine in a large bowl. Cut the chicken into bite-size pieces and add them to the bowl.

5. **Make the dressing:** In a small bowl, mash the anchovy with a fork or spoon until it's more of a chunky paste than a fillet. Add the lemon juice, mustard, Worcestershire, garlic, and pepper and keep mashing to break up the anchovy. Stir in the mayonnaise, Parmesan, and olive oil. I like a pretty thick dressing, but if you want, you can thin it by stirring in ½ teaspoon water at a time until it's just how you like it.

6. Drizzle a few tablespoons of the dressing over the greens and chicken and toss to coat. Taste and make sure there's enough dressing for you; if not, add more. Sprinkle the croutons and all crispy cheese bits from the baking sheet on top, then finish with the Parmesan. Serve with the lemon wedge on the side for squeezing over.

Crispy Rice Spicy Tuna

This sushi restaurant mainstay was created by Katsuya Uechi for his eponymous Los Angeles restaurant. Katsuya is an LA staple, and IYKYK but IYDKNYW (if you don't know, now you will). I first had it with my friend Flora, who *loves* crispy rice spicy tuna. And I love Flora, so here we are. This is something we always order and then eat and are too full to eat the actual meal, so this is a *perfect* single serving. Bricks of seasoned sushi rice are crisped in a pan and topped with a spicy, creamy raw tuna topping. This recipe makes nine bricks, which is a great and fancy meal. Or fry off half the bricks for a side dish to enjoy with a green salad, some edamame, or a tofu stir-fry, then save the rest of the bricks and tuna for another round tomorrow.

Serves 1 or 2

¾ cup sushi rice

2 teaspoons rice vinegar

1 teaspoon sugar

¾ teaspoon kosher salt

4 ounces sushi-grade raw tuna, finely chopped, or 1 (5-ounce) can tuna, drained

1 scallion, thinly sliced

1 tablespoon mayonnaise

2 teaspoons sriracha, plus more to taste

½ teaspoon soy sauce

2 tablespoons vegetable oil, such as canola, plus more for greasing

1 tablespoon unsalted butter

½ small avocado (see Note)

1. Place the rice in a small bowl and cover with cold water by 1 inch. Swish the rice around gently with your hand, then pour off the water. Repeat two or three times until the water is clear. Cover the rice with fresh water and soak for 30 minutes. Drain the rice and transfer it to a medium saucepan with a tight-fitting lid. Stir in 1 cup water, 1½ teaspoons of the vinegar, the sugar, and ½ teaspoon of the salt. Bring to a boil over high heat, then reduce the heat to low, cover, and cook until the rice is tender, 18 to 20 minutes. Remove from the heat and let stand, covered, for 10 minutes.

2. Line a loaf pan with plastic wrap, leaving a generous overhang on the long sides. Transfer the rice to the prepared pan and press it down into an even layer (don't press too hard or the rice will be very dense). Let stand at room temperature until cool, about 30 minutes, then cover tightly with the overhanging plastic wrap. Refrigerate until firm, at least 2 hours but preferably longer, up to 24 hours.

3. In a medium bowl, stir together the tuna, scallion, mayonnaise, sriracha, soy sauce, and remaining ½ teaspoon vinegar.

4. Unwrap the rice and invert it onto a cutting board. Remove the plastic wrap. Grease your knife with a bit of oil, then cut the rice into thirds lengthwise, then into thirds crosswise, so you have 9 even rectangles.

5. Heat the oil and butter in a large nonstick skillet over medium heat. Line a plate with paper towels and set it nearby. When the butter is foaming, add the rice blocks to the pan and cook until golden on the bottom, 5 to 10 minutes, then flip and cook until golden on the second side, 5 to 10 minutes more. Transfer to the paper towel–lined plate and sprinkle with the remaining ¼ teaspoon salt.

6. Thinly slice the avocado, then place 1 or 2 slices on top of each block of rice. Top each with a scant tablespoon of the spicy tuna and eat it up.

Note

What to do with the other avocado half, you ask???? Half an avocado is the ideal quantity to have staring at you in the fridge. This leftover is a gift, not a chore! Sprinkle it with everything bagel seasoning or furikake and eat it with a spoon, shingle it over toast, or add it to egg tacos.

Chicken Tabbou-Lee Daniels' *The Butler* Has the Night Off

Tabbouleh, pronounced tub-*boo*-lee, is a popular Middle Eastern couscous-based salad that I love to make when I haven't had a vegetable in a while. The za'atar-seasoned chicken gives this an extra bit of flavor that pairs well with the salad's herbs and lemon. It's a simple, easy meal to make when your butler takes the night off.

Serves 1

Couscous Salad

¼ cup uncooked couscous

¼ cup boiling water

Kosher salt and freshly ground black pepper

½ cup chopped fresh flat-leaf parsley

1 small Roma tomato, chopped (¼ cup)

1 small English cucumber, chopped (2 tablespoons)

½ small red onion or 1 scallion, thinly sliced (1 tablespoon)

1 tablespoon extra-virgin olive oil

1 tablespoon fresh lemon juice (from about ½ lemon)

Chicken

1 small boneless, skinless chicken breast (5 to 6 ounces)

Kosher salt and freshly ground black pepper

Pinch of ground za'atar or cumin (optional)

½ teaspoon extra-virgin olive oil

1. **Make the couscous:** In a small heatproof bowl, combine the couscous, boiling water, and a pinch of salt. Cover with a small plate and let the couscous steam for 5 minutes. Uncover, fluff with a fork, and set aside to cool.

2. **Meanwhile, make the chicken:** Season the chicken with salt, pepper, and za'atar (if using). Heat the olive oil in a small skillet over medium heat. When shimmering, cook the chicken until golden brown and cooked through, 5 to 6 minutes per side. Transfer to a plate to let rest for 5 minutes, then slice thinly.

3. In a medium bowl, combine the parsley, tomato, cucumber, onion, olive oil, and couscous. Add the lemon juice. Season with salt and pepper and toss to combine.

4. Spoon the couscous salad into a shallow bowl and top with the sliced chicken. Serve warm or at room temperature.

Peanut Noodles

I wouldn't consider this a traditional "salad," per se, but it's cold and it has vegetables, so it counts. A favorite for PB-heads, this is relatively quick, and the peanuts on top make for a nice crunchy crunch, like the sound my dog, Peanut, makes when she eats her kibble. If you're as clumsy with a knife as I am, this is the time to bring out your julienne peeler to make veggie matchsticks, which will blend nicely into the noodles.

Serves 1 generously

Peanut Sauce

3 tablespoons creamy peanut butter

1 tablespoon fresh lime juice (from about 1 lime)

1 tablespoon soy sauce

1 to 3 tablespoons sriracha or chile paste, to taste

1 teaspoon toasted sesame oil

1 teaspoon maple syrup (optional; use only if your peanut butter is unsweetened)

1 (½-inch) piece fresh ginger, peeled and grated

1 garlic clove, grated

Noodles

3 ounces dried wheat noodles (such as ramen, somen, lo mein, or spaghetti)

2 teaspoons kosher salt

1 cup finely shredded red cabbage or bagged slaw mix

1 Persian (mini) cucumber, cut into 2-inch matchsticks

1 medium carrot, cut into 2-inch matchsticks

2 scallions, cut into 2-inch sections, then sliced lengthwise

¼ cup cilantro sprigs, coarsely chopped

1 tablespoon finely chopped roasted peanuts

½ lime, cut into wedges, for serving

1. **Make the sauce:** In a small bowl, use a fork to whisk together the peanut butter, lime juice, soy sauce, sriracha, sesame oil, maple syrup (if using), ginger, and garlic until smooth. You want a thick yet pourable sauce, so add water 1 teaspoon at a time if it's *too* thick.

2. **Make the noodles:** Bring 4 cups water to a boil in a small pot over medium-high heat. Add the noodles and salt and cook according to the package directions. Drain the noodles, then rinse them with cold water to stop the cooking. Shake off any excess water, then place the noodles in a large bowl and add the cabbage, cucumber, carrot, scallions, and cilantro. Drizzle with about half the peanut sauce and toss, making sure everything is well coated. Taste and add more peanut sauce if you think it needs it (it always does).

3. Sprinkle with the peanuts and eat with the lime wedges alongside for squeezing.

Caprese Salad with Crispy Prosciutto

While I love a regular caprese salad, there's a way to make it better, and that's by throwing crisped ham in it. The ingredients call for four prosciutto slices, but I'd grab five or six from the fridge, because much like a little piggy, you might pork your way through it before the salad is even done. (If you're a big "nah" on ham, though, feel free to leave out the prosciutto.)

Serves 1

1 ripe medium tomato (choose one that smells great—that's a sign of flavor), thickly sliced

¼ teaspoon flaky salt or kosher salt

⅛ teaspoon sugar

Pinch of freshly ground black pepper

½ (8-ounce) ball fresh mozzarella, torn into bite-size pieces, or ½ (8-ounce) container mozzarella pearls, drained

2 teaspoons plus 1 tablespoon extra-virgin olive oil

4 slices prosciutto

1 teaspoon balsamic vinegar

¼ cup loosely packed fresh basil leaves

Good crusty bread, such as sourdough, for serving

1. Place the tomato slices on a dinner plate and sprinkle the salt, sugar, and pepper evenly over both sides. Toss the tomatoes once with your hand to help distribute the seasonings, then arrange the slices in a single layer on the plate. Arrange the mozzarella around the tomato slices.

2. Line a small plate with paper towels. Heat 2 teaspoons of the olive oil in a medium skillet over medium heat until it shimmers. Add the prosciutto and cook, undisturbed, until it shrinks and is mostly golden on the bottom, 2 to 3 minutes, then flip and cook until golden on the second side, about 2 minutes more. Transfer the prosciutto to the paper towel–lined plate to drain and cool for a few minutes.

3. Drizzle the tomatoes and mozzarella with the remaining 1 tablespoon oil and the vinegar. Crumble the crispy prosciutto over the salad, then tear the basil leaves over everything. Eat right away, with bread to soak up the juices.

Fancy Fish Niçoise

I didn't know that "Niçoise" as an adjective describes something from Nice in France, but it does, and now you know, too. A Niçoise salad is typically very shopping-heavy: so many ingredients to buy, then use just part of, then figure out what to do with the rest of. It's very French in that way. This recipe streamlines the selection and makes it a feasible process for any night. Instead of cooking fish, this salad uses tinned fish and adds a little . . . je ne sais quoi, but the *quoi* in question is tinned fish, which is fancier than your regular can of tuna. You may never get to the Cannes Film Festival—hell, neither will I—but you can still have a little slice of the South of France at home!

Serves 1

2 baby Yukon Gold or red potatoes (about 2 inches each), or a handful of fingerling potatoes

Kosher salt

Small handful of green beans (about 10 beans), trimmed

1 large egg

3 tablespoons extra-virgin olive oil

1 tablespoon red wine vinegar or fresh lemon juice

1 teaspoon Dijon mustard

1 head Little Gem lettuce, leaves separated, larger leaves torn

1 (4-ounce) tin oil-packed sardines, mackerel, or other fish, drained

1 tablespoon chopped pitted Kalamata or Niçoise olives

1. Place the potatoes in a medium saucepan and fill with cold water to cover by 1 inch. Season the water with salt and taste it—make sure it's salty like broth so it'll season the potatoes. Bring to a boil over high heat and cook until the potatoes are fork-tender, 10 to 15 minutes (if you're using fingerlings, start checking them after 5 minutes). Transfer to a plate with a slotted spoon.

2. Add the green beans to the boiling water and cook until they are tender but still have some bite, 2 to 3 minutes. Using the slotted spoon, transfer them to the plate with the potatoes.

3. Add the egg to the boiling water and boil for 7½ minutes. Meanwhile, fill a small bowl with ice and water. Use the slotted spoon to transfer the egg to the bowl of ice water to cool, then peel the egg.

4. In a medium bowl, stir together the olive oil, vinegar, mustard, and a pinch of salt.

5. Press down on the potatoes with a spoon to break them in half, then add them to the bowl with the dressing. Add the green beans and toss to coat.

6. Arrange the lettuce on a plate and sprinkle it lightly with salt. Top with the potatoes and green beans, fish, and olives. Rip the egg in half and add that, too. Spoon any dressing left in the bowl over the salad, then eat right away.

Taste the Rainbow Roll

One of the perks of being a movie writer is something called a roundtable, which is when a studio or producer hires a handful of writers for a day or a couple days to make some tweaks to an existing script. It's a nice way to meet other writers but more importantly, you get a free lunch and 9 out of 10 times it's sushi because it's expensive and even more delicious when someone else paid for it! (I think I only became a writer because there are so many opportunities for free lunch.) Sadly, those lunches don't happen every day, so this two-roll recipe is a great substitute for fancy sushi at home. Honey, get out the sushi mat! We're rollin' here!! Placing the fish on top is not traditionally Japanese; it's an American twist. You can get sushi-grade fish from the sushi counter at a grocery store or at a fishmonger. Tell them you're making a rainbow roll, which is called that both because it is an ally and because of the colorful pattern of the ingredients.

Makes 2 rolls

¾ cup sushi rice (see Note page 66)

¼ teaspoon kosher salt

4 ounces sushi-grade tuna or salmon (or a mix, if you're feeling fancy)

2 tablespoons seasoned rice vinegar

2 ounces imitation crab or drained canned crabmeat

2 to 3 teaspoons mayonnaise, as needed

½ ripe but firm avocado

1 lemon wedge

2 (8-inch) nori sheets

½ Persian (mini) cucumber, cut lengthwise into long, thin matchsticks

For Serving

Soy sauce

Pickled ginger

Wasabi

1. Place the rice in a small bowl and cover with cold water by 1 inch. Swish the rice around gently with your hand, then pour off the water. Repeat two or three times until the water runs clear. Cover the rice with fresh water and soak for 30 minutes, then drain.

2. Place the rice in a small saucepan and add ¾ cup plus 2 tablespoons water and the salt. Flip the lid of the pot upside down and wrap it in aluminum foil (this will create a tight seal between the pot and lid to prevent any steam from escaping—just make sure the foil comes up and over the sides). Bring the water to a gentle boil over medium heat, then reduce the heat to low, cover the pan with the foil-wrapped lid, and cook for 16 minutes. Remove from the heat and let the rice steam, still covered, for 10 minutes.

3. Meanwhile, place the fish in the freezer for 20 to 30 minutes to make it easier to slice.

4. Transfer the cooked rice to a large, wide bowl. Sprinkle the vinegar all over, then, using a wooden spoon or wide spatula, fold the vinegar into the rice by scooping from one edge of the bowl up through the middle, then turning the bowl a quarter turn (this cools the rice and helps it absorb the vinegar). Repeat until the rice has cooled to room temperature, 3 to 4 minutes. Cover the bowl with a damp kitchen towel.

Recipe continues

5. Pat the crab dry. If it isn't already cut into slices, cut it into 1-inch pieces, then shred the meat with your fingers. Place it in a small bowl and stir in 2 teaspoons of the mayonnaise. If the mixture looks dry to you, add another teaspoon. Remove the fish from the freezer and put it on your cutting board with the grain (the lines in the flesh) parallel to you. Slice the fish at an angle against the grain into the thinnest and longest slices you can manage. Cut the avocado lengthwise the same way (super thin) and squeeze a few drops of lemon juice over it to keep it green.

6. Fill a small bowl with warm water. Lay one nori sheet on your work surface with one longer side closest to you (and shiny-side up) and scoop half the rice onto the nori. Dampen your fingers with the warm water and use them to spread the rice in an even layer all the way to the edges of the nori. Cover the rice with plastic wrap, then lay a sushi mat on top of it. Carefully flip everything so the plastic is against the sushi mat, the rice is under the nori, and the nori is on top. Make sure the mat is positioned so you can roll away from you.

7. Place half the cucumber slices in a thin line one-third of the way up the sheet of nori. Arrange half the crab mixture next to it, closer to you. Starting with the end closest to you, lift the sushi mat and plastic and roll the nori until you've enclosed the fillings and squeeze to make sure it's firm. Keep rolling, lifting the plastic up as you go, until the entire sheet is formed into a tight roll. Set the finished roll aside and make one more with the remaining nori, rice, cucumber, and crab. Save the sheet of plastic.

8. Starting at one end of a roll, drape a piece of the fish diagonally over the top. Slightly overlap it with a slice of avocado, just so no rice is exposed, then repeat, alternating fish and avocado, until you've covered the whole roll. Do the same for the other roll. Depending on how thin you were able to cut your fish, you may have some extra. Sashimi!

9. Place the plastic wrap over the sushi roll with the dirty side up. Dampen your sharpest chef's knife and cut the roll into 6 to 8 slices each through the plastic (this helps keep everything neat), rewetting the knife between each cut. Remove the plastic and arrange the slices on a serving plate. Serve with a small bowl of soy sauce, some pickled ginger, and a bit of wasabi.

Note

If you have a rice cooker and want to use that, soak and cook 1 cup of sushi rice with 1 cup plus 3 tablespoons water. Use 2 cups of the cooked rice and save any extra for another meal.

Cheesy

& Gooey

Leave Me Alone Lasagna

Ah, one of the recipes that was the impetus for this cookbook. I love lasagna. And what's not to love? Long pieces of noodle layered with simmering sauce, meat, and cheese. Oh, the cheese. So melty. Again, I love lasagna. But I do not love eating lasagna every night for a week. This single-ish serving fills your 'gna need with minimal ingredients and by creatively replacing ground beef with sausage. Making a small batch means you get all the comfort without the commitment. Sharing is optional, but I won't judge if you want to be left alone.

Serves 2

Nonstick cooking spray for greasing

1 teaspoon extra-virgin olive oil

2 sweet or hot Italian sausages, casings removed

1 cup of your favorite marinara sauce

¼ teaspoon kosher salt, plus more if needed

¼ teaspoon freshly ground black pepper

6 oven-ready or no-boil lasagna sheets

1 (8-ounce) ball fresh mozzarella, quartered

½ cup freshly and finely grated Parmigiano Reggiano cheese

1. Preheat the oven to 400°F. You'll need an 8½ × 4½-inch loaf pan or small baking dish (about 6½ × 5 inches) for the lasagna. If it isn't nonstick, coat it lightly with nonstick spray.

2. Heat the olive oil in a medium skillet over medium heat for 1 minute. Add a small piece of sausage to the pan—if it sizzles immediately, the oil is hot enough; if not, wait a minute and try again. Add all the sausage and break it apart with a spoon or spatula into very small pieces. Cook, continuing to break up the sausage, until browned and cooked through, about 5 minutes. Pour in the marinara sauce and ¼ cup water, add the salt and pepper, then stir and bring to a simmer. Taste; depending on your sauce, it may need a little more salt. The sauce should be well seasoned because the noodles are not! Remove from the heat.

3. Spread 2 tablespoons of the meat sauce over the bottom of the prepared pan. Add a layer of lasagna noodles, breaking them up as needed so they fit in a single layer with no overlap. Spoon ⅓ cup of the sauce over the noodles, spreading it all the way to the edges. Rip one-quarter of the mozzarella into small pieces and scatter them over the sauce in an even layer, then sprinkle 2 tablespoons of the Parmesan on top. Repeat this layering process three more times, using the remaining sauce, noodles, mozzarella, and Parm. Make sure the top layer of noodles is covered in sauce to help it cook, and if you have more than ⅓ cup of sauce left, just pour it all on and let it seep down the sides. Depending on the size of your pan, you might not need 6 lasagna sheets; if your pan is just an inch or so tall, the lasagna will be taller than the rim now, but it will collapse as it bakes.

4. Coat a piece of aluminum foil with nonstick spray. Cover the pan tightly with the foil, sprayed-side down, then place it on a small baking sheet to catch any drips. Bake for 20 minutes, then check the lasagna: If the sauce is steadily bubbling around the edges, remove the foil. If not, cover and bake for 5 minutes more, then check again. Bake, uncovered, for 10 to 15 minutes more, until the cheese is browned and bubbly on top. Remove from the oven and let stand for 15 to 20 minutes to set, then cut the lasagna into squares and serve.

Say No to Drugs Jalapeño Poppers

At the end of a tense day, these jalapeño poppers are guaranteed to loosen you up. The cream cheese layer mixed with those dank jalapeños, wrapped in bacon, will put you on cloud nine. And whipping out the air fryer to cook them instead of getting baked will leave you feeling greasy-guilt-free.

Serves 1

2 (3- to 4-inch) fresh jalapeños

3 tablespoons shredded sharp cheddar cheese

2 tablespoons cream cheese, at room temperature

2 pickled jalapeño slices, finely chopped

Pinch of kosher salt

Pinch of freshly ground black pepper

Pinch of smoked paprika

2 slices bacon, halved lengthwise

1. Cut the jalapeños in half lengthwise through the stems. Use a spoon or your knife to scrape out the seeds and any white membranes (that's where the heat is!).

2. In a small bowl, stir together the cheddar, cream cheese, pickled jalapeño slices, salt, pepper, and paprika until well combined. Divide the cheese mixture among the jalapeño halves, spreading it evenly from end to end and level with the top of the jalapeño (the filling will puff up as it cooks).

3. Loosely wrap each stuffed jalapeño with a strip of bacon. Place them on the rack in the air fryer and air-fry at 400°F for 8 to 10 minutes, until the bacon is crisp and browned. Let cool for 5 minutes before eating.

Note

If you don't have an air fryer, preheat the oven to 400°F. Line a baking sheet with aluminum foil, then set a wire rack on top. Place the bacon-wrapped jalapeños on the prepared baking sheet and bake for 20 to 25 minutes, until the bacon is crisp and browned.

Note
Save the other half
of the dough ball for
the breadsticks
on page 87.

Stuck in the Friend Calzone

We've all been there. You love them, they love you . . . but only as a friend. In your head you'd make the perfect couple, and the other person just doesn't see it. Technically, the friend zone isn't real because it implies you should aspire to continue harassing someone into loving you back (you can't, I've tried). But for all intents and purposes, this calzone is full of enough love, and cheese, to make you forget all about them. Who needs requited love when you have a sauced-on-top calzone? Not you, honey! This recipe is for a regular cheese calzone, but I've included other filling options so you can stuff your individual calzone to your wildest dreams.

Makes 1

- 2 teaspoons extra-virgin olive oil, plus more for greasing
- ½ (8-ounce) ball store-bought pizza dough (see Note)
- 1 cup shredded low-moisture mozzarella cheese
- 2 tablespoons freshly and finely grated Parmigiano Reggiano cheese
- ¼ teaspoon dried oregano
- ⅛ teaspoon red pepper flakes, or to taste
- ⅛ teaspoon garlic powder
- ½ cup of your favorite marinara sauce, or more if you love sauce

1. Preheat the oven to 450°F. Line a baking sheet with parchment paper, then lightly oil the parchment. Cover the dough ball with a damp kitchen towel and let it stand at room temperature for 30 minutes while the oven heats.

2. Place the dough ball on the prepared baking sheet. Starting at the center, push the dough outward, rotating it a quarter turn after each push, until you have a roughly 8-inch round. If the dough is fighting you and springs back as you're shaping it, cover it and let it rest for 10 minutes, then try again.

3. Fill a small bowl with water. In a separate small bowl, mix the mozzarella, 1 tablespoon of the Parmesan, the oregano, red pepper flakes, and garlic powder and toss to combine. Sprinkle the cheese mixture over half the dough, leaving a ½-inch border around the edge. Spoon 2 tablespoons of the marinara over the cheese mixture. Dip a finger in the bowl of water and use it to dampen the edges of the dough, then fold the empty half over to encase the sauce and cheese and pinch the edges together to seal. Brush the top of the calzone with the olive oil. Spread a heaping spoonful of the marinara over the top, then sprinkle with the remaining 1 tablespoon Parmesan.

4. Bake for 15 to 18 minutes, until the crust is golden brown. Meanwhile, heat the remaining marinara sauce in a small saucepan over low heat, stirring continuously, until it's steaming.

5. Remove the calzone from the oven and let it rest on the pan for 5 minutes, then serve, with the warm marinara on the side for dipping.

Filling Variations

Pepperoni Calzone: Lay 6 slices of pepperoni over the cheese and sauce in a single layer before closing the dough and bake as directed.

Spinach Calzone: Reduce the mozzarella to ½ cup. Thaw ½ (10-ounce) package of frozen spinach, then squeeze out all the excess water (this may take a few tries). Add the spinach to the bowl with the cheese mixture, stir to combine, and continue as directed.

The "Stupid Good" Sicilian Square

As a Chicagoan, pizza in my cookbook was inevitable. I forwent (did you know this is the past tense of the word *forgo*???) my deep-dish roots to opt for something a little easier and almost as delicious and cheesy as getting it in a restaurant—and behold, the Sicilian square! This version stays simple with mozzarella, an oniony tomato sauce, and Parmesan cheese (layered in that order so the sauce doesn't sog the crust). This is the ideal "It's Friday night but my pants are already off so I'm staying in" meal, and after taking a bite and tasting that onion sauce, you'll turn to no one and say, "That is stupid good."

Serves 1

4 tablespoons extra-virgin olive oil

1 (8-ounce) ball store-bought pizza dough, at room temperature (see Note)

1 small yellow onion, thinly sliced

Kosher salt

3 tablespoons tomato paste

¾ cup shredded low-moisture mozzarella cheese (3 ounces)

¼ cup freshly and finely grated Parmigiano Reggiano cheese (1 ounce)

1. Preheat the oven to 450°F.

2. Pour 2 tablespoons of the olive oil into an 8-inch square baking pan. Add the pizza dough and stretch and dimple it to fit the pan, turning the dough to coat it in the oil. If the dough is fighting you and springs back as you're shaping it, cover it and let it rest for 10 minutes, then try again. Bake for 10 to 12 minutes, until the crust is barely golden on top.

3. Meanwhile, in a medium saucepan, heat the remaining 2 tablespoons olive oil over medium heat. Add the onion and a pinch of salt and cook, stirring often, until softened, 3 to 5 minutes. Add the tomato paste and cook, stirring, until the paste is a shade darker and starts to stick to the bottom of the pot, 3 to 5 minutes. Add ½ cup water and a pinch of salt and simmer until the sauce is thickened and flavorful, 3 to 5 minutes. Remove from the heat.

4. Remove the crust from the oven and top it with the mozzarella, then the sauce, then the Parmesan. Return the pizza to the oven and bake until all the cheese has melted and the sides of the crust are golden, 5 to 10 minutes. Remove from the oven and let rest for a few minutes before eating.

Note

D'oh! Extra dough? Trader Joe's now sells pizza dough! Hooray! But if you grab fresh dough from your pizza place instead, it'll likely come in a 16-ounce blob, which you can freeze half for future you. Future you will also love you for picking up a tube of tomato paste: Not only is it double-concentrated, which means doubly tomatoey, it's easier to store than a can and lasts longer.

Chicken Parm Nuggets

Every recipe for this classic Italian comfort food is batched for 1,000 people. Every recipe, except this version. Funny story: One time when I was making this for dinner, I forgot to buy the mozzarella ball and had to use shredded cheese, which I do not recommend if you want a yummy, gooey, golden cheese top. I suffered so you don't have to. These are easy bite-size nuggets you'll say you'll save for later but will eat before bed.

Serves 1 generously

¼ cup all-purpose flour

1 large egg

½ cup panko breadcrumbs

4 tablespoons freshly and finely grated Parmigiano Reggiano cheese

½ teaspoon kosher salt

¼ teaspoon dried oregano

⅛ teaspoon freshly ground black pepper

1 (8-ounce) boneless, skinless chicken breast

2 tablespoons extra-virgin olive oil

¾ cup of your favorite marinara sauce

½ (8-ounce) ball fresh mozzarella cheese, cut into 6 slices

1. Place the flour on a small plate. Crack the egg into a shallow bowl and whisk with a fork until no streaks of egg white remain. In another small shallow bowl, stir together the panko, 2 tablespoons of the Parmesan, ¼ teaspoon of the salt, the oregano, and half the pepper.

2. Lay the chicken on a piece of plastic wrap large enough to fold back over the chicken or put it in a gallon-size zip-top bag. Using a meat mallet, rolling pin, or the bottom of a sturdy pot, pound the chicken to an even ½-inch or so thickness—you're not looking for it to be super thin, just even. Season the chicken all over with the remaining ¼ teaspoon salt and remaining black pepper, then cut it into 6 equal pieces.

3. Working one piece at a time, dip the chicken in the flour to coat, then shake off any excess. Dip it in the egg to coat completely, letting any excess egg drip off, then place it in the breadcrumb mixture, pressing it lightly to help the crumbs stick and making sure it's evenly and completely coated. Transfer the breaded chicken to a plate and repeat with the remaining pieces.

4. Heat the olive oil in a medium skillet over medium heat for 1 minute. Add a pinch of flour to the pan—if it sizzles immediately, the oil is hot enough; if not, wait a minute and try again. Add all the breaded chicken pieces to the pan and cook until they're golden brown all over, about 3 minutes per side. (Don't worry about cooking them through—they'll finish in the oven.) Transfer the nuggets to a plate.

5. Meanwhile, position a rack 6 inches from the broiler heating element and preheat the broiler to high.

6. Spread ¼ cup of the marinara over the bottom of a small baking pan (an 8-inch square pan or a 9 × 7-inch pan works well). Arrange the nuggets in a single layer over the sauce, then top each nugget with a slice of mozzarella. Pour the remaining ½ cup sauce over the nuggets, then sprinkle the top with the remaining 2 tablespoons Parmesan.

7. Broil for 10 to 12 minutes, until the sauce is bubbling, cheese is lightly browned in spots, and the chicken is cooked through; check regularly, as every broiler is different. Remove from the oven and let cool for 5 minutes before eating.

No Emoji, Eggplant Parm

Hey, vegetarian friends, did you just read the Chicken Parm Nuggets recipe (page 79) and salivate, but then get sad 'cause you couldn't eat them? No need to be green with envy—this is especially for you! Slicing the eggplant lengthwise will give it a little aesthetic variety compared to traditional eggplant Parm rounds. If you can find smaller eggplants (such as Japanese eggplants), I'd recommend you get those instead of the big boys, because it'll be 59 percent tastier, a number I made up. So filling, you won't need to send those eggplant + water droplet emojis to people anymore. (That's what that means, right? Eggplants + water droplets = "salivating for eggplant Parm"?)

Serves 1

3 tablespoons extra-virgin olive oil, plus more for greasing

2 Italian eggplants (about 4 ounces each), or 1 small globe eggplant (about 1 pound)

¼ teaspoon kosher salt

¼ teaspoon freshly ground black pepper

¼ cup panko breadcrumbs

3 tablespoons freshly and finely grated Parmigiano Reggiano cheese

½ cup of your favorite marinara sauce

⅓ cup shredded low-moisture mozzarella cheese

6 small or 3 large basil leaves, for garnish

1. Preheat the oven to 425°F. Grease a small baking sheet with olive oil.
2. Cut off the tops of the eggplant(s), then halve them lengthwise (if you're using one large eggplant, save half for another meal). Stand one eggplant up with the trimmed (flat) side on the cutting board to steady it and carefully cut about ¼ inch of the skin side off, lengthwise, so you have a thin, wide plank of eggplant with flesh exposed on two flat sides. Repeat with all the pieces. (If you're using a large eggplant, you should have one flat but thick plank. Cut it in half lengthwise to make two thinner planks.)
3. Place the eggplant slices on the prepared baking sheet and drizzle the tops evenly with 1 tablespoon of the olive oil, rubbing it in to make sure the slices are evenly coated. Flip the slices and drizzle the second side evenly with 1 tablespoon of the olive oil. Season the slices all over with the salt and pepper.
4. Bake the eggplant for 15 to 20 minutes, until the bottoms are golden, then flip and bake until golden on the second side and tender, 5 to 10 minutes more. Remove the eggplant from the oven but keep the oven on.
5. In a small bowl, stir together the breadcrumbs, Parmesan, and remaining 1 tablespoon olive oil until evenly combined.
6. Divide the marinara among the eggplant slices and spread it in an even layer, then evenly sprinkle the mozzarella over the eggplant. Finally, divide the breadcrumb mixture evenly among the slices.
7. Bake for 5 to 8 minutes, until the sauce is bubbling, the cheese is melted, and the breadcrumbs are browned. Remove from the oven and let cool for 5 minutes. Tear the basil leaves over top before digging in.

Quiche Lorrenzo

Lorraine, Lorraine, Lorraine. Everyone's always talking about Lorraine, but no one ever talks about Lorrenzo. Probably because unlike the Lorraine region in France, the namesake for the quiche Lorraine, Lorrenzo doesn't exist. But that's not a reason to ignore him. The famous Lorraine's forgotten Italian half-sibling, the Lorrenzo, is a savory, flaky way to start your solo morning.

Serves 1 or 2

- 1 disk store-bought pie dough, thawed if necessary but kept cold
- ¼ cup finely chopped pancetta or bacon
- 1 medium shallot, thinly sliced
- 2 large eggs
- ½ cup half-and-half
- ¼ teaspoon kosher salt
- ⅛ teaspoon freshly ground black pepper
- ⅓ cup freshly grated Fontina or Gruyère cheese
- 1 tablespoon freshly and finely grated Parmigiano Reggiano cheese

1. Preheat the oven to 400°F. Pull out a small baking dish, either a roughly 6½ × 5-inch rectangular one or a round one that holds 1½ to 2 cups.

2. Unroll the pie dough on your work surface and cut it into a rectangle that is 3 inches larger than the bottom of your baking dish (for a 6½ × 5-inch baking dish, that will be 9½ × 8 inches; if you have to cut a slightly smaller rectangle than that, or some of the corners are rounded, that's fine). Gently drape the dough over the baking dish, easing it into the bottom corners and taking care to hold the edges gently so you don't tear the dough. Fold the overhanging dough around the edges in and under itself, then use your thumb and index finger to crimp it, making sure the dough is pressed against the edge of the baking dish (this helps with shrinking). Prick the bottom a few times with a fork and freeze the crust for 10 minutes while you prepare the filling.

3. In a small skillet, cook the pancetta (or bacon!) and the shallot over medium heat, stirring occasionally and adjusting the heat if the shallot starts to stick, until the pancetta is browned and crisp and the shallot is softened, 6 to 8 minutes total. Remove from the heat and let cool.

4. Remove the crust from the freezer, line it with a piece of parchment paper or aluminum foil, and fill it halfway to the top with either dried beans or uncooked rice. Bake for 10 minutes, then carefully remove the parchment and beans or rice and bake for 7 to 10 minutes more, until the bottom is lightly golden. Remove the crust from the oven but keep the oven on.

5. In a medium bowl, whisk together the eggs, half-and-half, salt, and pepper until no streaks of egg white remain. Add the Fontina, Parmesan, and cooled pancetta mixture, leaving any grease in the pan, and stir to combine. Pour the mixture into the baked crust.

6. Bake for 25 to 30 minutes, until the filling is set but still just slightly jiggly in the center. If the crust is getting too browned for your liking before the filling is done, loosely cover the crust with foil. Remove the quiche from the oven and let cool on a wire rack for at least 10 minutes or up to 30 minutes before serving.

S'Mac Talk and Cheese

Macaroni and cheese . . . a side dish known for inciting fights at the dinner table because people have feelings on it. Should there be crumbs on top? How many cheeses is *too* many? Does the best version come from a box? A person's choice of mac and cheese is a personal one, so eating it in the company of others is kindling for heavy smack talk. I'm saving you the trouble: One serving of a neutral, cheesy mac and cheese to spare you from your aunties cussing each other out over who brought the best version.

Serves 1 generously

½ cup half-and-half or whole milk

1 tablespoon unsalted butter

1 teaspoon kosher salt

½ teaspoon mustard powder

¼ teaspoon freshly ground black pepper

¼ teaspoon garlic powder or onion powder (or ⅛ teaspoon of each)

Pinch of cayenne pepper (optional)

1 cup elbow macaroni

½ cup freshly grated sharp cheddar cheese (2 ounces; see Note)

½ cup freshly grated Gruyère cheese (2 ounces)

3 tablespoons freshly and finely grated Parmigiano Reggiano cheese

¼ teaspoon cornstarch

2 tablespoons panko breadcrumbs

1. In a medium saucepan, combine 1 cup water, the half-and-half, butter, salt, mustard powder, black pepper, garlic powder, and cayenne (if using). Bring to a boil over medium heat, stirring often, then add the macaroni, reduce the heat to medium-low, and cook, stirring often so nothing sticks to the bottom of the pot, until the pasta is al dente, 10 to 12 minutes. The pasta should be just barely covered by the liquid, and it won't look saucy, but that's okay!

2. Meanwhile, position a rack in the center of the oven and preheat the broiler to high.

3. In a small bowl, combine the cheddar, Gruyère, 1 tablespoon of the Parmesan, and the cornstarch and toss to combine.

4. Back to the pasta: Reduce the heat to low and, while stirring continuously, add the cheese mixture one large pinch at a time, stirring until the cheese has melted and the sauce is smooth before adding the next pinch, 1 to 2 minutes total. Transfer the pasta mixture to a small (2-cup or a little bigger) baking dish.

5. In a small bowl (you can use the one for the cheese to save on dishes), stir together the breadcrumbs and remaining 2 tablespoons Parmesan. Sprinkle the topping over the pasta mixture. Broil for 2 to 3 minutes, until the topping is browned and the sauce is bubbling (every broiler is different, so watch carefully). Remove the baking dish from the oven and let cool for 5 minutes before digging in.

A Cheese Note

Grate the cheese yourself, as the preshredded stuff has anticlumping additives that will prevent you from achieving a truly creamy sauce. Use the biggest holes on a box grater for the cheddar and Gruyère and the smallest holes for the Parm.

"I'm Stuffed" Breadsticks

To say I love Domino's cheesy breadsticks is an understatement. How much do I love them? I love them so much that after finishing the New York City Marathon in 2022, my first and only meal was Domino's. For a glorious six months in my midtwenties, in addition to my day job as an assistant, I worked at Domino's delivering pizzas. I had hoped to make extra money to pay off some credit card debt, but who are we kidding . . . it was for the free pizza and breadsticks. This is an homage to my love for Domino's, and should you feel compelled to eat them all in one sitting (do not do that), you will feel as stuffed as the breadsticks.

Serves 1 or 2

½ (8-ounce) ball store-bought pizza dough (see Note)

All-purpose flour, for dusting

½ cup shredded low-moisture mozzarella cheese

½ cup shredded cheddar cheese

2 tablespoons freshly and finely grated Parmigiano Reggiano cheese

1 tablespoon unsalted butter

¼ teaspoon garlic powder

¼ teaspoon Italian seasoning or dried oregano

¼ teaspoon kosher salt

1. Preheat the oven to 400°F. Line a baking sheet with parchment paper. Cover the dough ball with a damp kitchen towel and let it stand at room temperature for 30 minutes while the oven heats.

2. Lightly flour your work surface and a rolling pin. Roll out the dough into an 8-inch square. If the dough is fighting you and springs back as you're shaping it, cover it and let it rest for 10 minutes, then try again.

3. Fill a small bowl with water. In a separate small bowl, mix the mozzarella, cheddar, and Parmesan. Spread about three-quarters of the cheese mixture over half the dough, leaving a ½-inch border all around. Dip a finger in the bowl of water and use it to dampen the edges of the dough, then fold the empty half over to encase the cheese and pinch the edges together to seal. Transfer the stuffed dough to the prepared baking sheet.

4. In a small bowl, combine the butter, garlic powder, Italian seasoning, and salt. Microwave the butter mixture in 15-second bursts until melted, a minute or so total. (Alternatively, combine the ingredients in a small saucepan and heat over medium-low heat until melted.) Brush the butter mixture generously over the stuffed dough. Cutting perpendicular to the long edge, slice the dough into 1-inch-wide sections, cutting almost all the way through but leaving the sections attached. Sprinkle with the remaining cheese mixture.

5. Bake the breadsticks for 17 to 20 minutes, until the dough is golden brown on the edges and the cheese has melted. Remove from the oven and let cool for 5 minutes, then pull the breadsticks apart and eat!

Note

Save the other half of the dough ball for the calzone on page 75.

Carby

& Cozy

No-Hangover Vodka Pasta

I present to you another go-to of mine that inspired this cookbook. I spent most of my time during the pandemic up in the San Bernadino Mountain area, far from LA and my beloved Jon & Vinny's vodka pasta. While I was cooped up alone, I did my best to satisfy my vodka pasta craving. But every recipe I found was to feed a family of ten, and by the third night, I never wanted to eat it again. It was very much like the vodka-induced hangovers I had in college. After nights of binge drinking, I'd swear I would never drink again, but then Friday would roll around and yours truly would once again be ripping shots at the bar. Thankfully, I eventually learned the concept of moderation, which now applies to both my shot-taking and my pasta-eating.

Serves 1

2½ teaspoons kosher salt

4 ounces tube-shaped pasta, such as rigatoni, penne, or paccheri

1 tablespoon unsalted butter

1 heaping tablespoon tomato paste

1 large or 2 small garlic cloves, grated or minced

¼ teaspoon sugar

⅛ teaspoon dried oregano

⅛ teaspoon red pepper flakes (optional)

2 tablespoons vodka

⅓ cup heavy cream

2 tablespoons freshly and finely grated Parmigiano Reggiano cheese

6 small or 3 large fresh basil leaves

1. Bring 4 cups water to a boil in a small pot over high heat. Add 2 teaspoons of the salt, then stir in the pasta and cook according to the package directions until al dente. Scoop out about ¼ cup of the pasta cooking water and set aside, then drain the pasta.

2. Meanwhile, in a small skillet, melt the butter over medium heat. Add the tomato paste, garlic, remaining ½ teaspoon salt, the sugar, oregano, and red pepper flakes (if using). Cook, stirring continuously, until the tomato paste has darkened a few shades and smells cooked, about 2 minutes. Remove the pan from the heat. While stirring continuously, pour in the vodka to incorporate it into the tomato paste. Stir in the cream until the sauce is a smooth orange color.

3. When the pasta is done, return the sauce to medium heat. Add the drained pasta and a splash (call it 1 tablespoon) of the reserved pasta cooking water. Shake the pan and stir aggressively—or toss it, if you're feeling brave—to mix everything together and emulsify the sauce. You're looking for a thick, glossy sauce that clings to and evenly coats the pasta. If the sauce is too thick, add another splash of pasta water. If it's too thin, let it simmer for a few minutes to thicken.

4. Transfer the sauced pasta to a serving dish, top with the cheese, and tear the basil over the top. Eat right away!

Gnocchi with Sausage and Peppas

Y'ALL, this is a sleeper hit. Your girl doesn't even like peppers (because, you know, flavor), but I gobbled this up. I tested the recipe at 11 p.m. and meant to only have one bite, but I ate the whole damn thing. The crisped gnocchi combined with the sausage-y sautéed peppers and onion will surprise you.

Serves 1 generously

2 tablespoons extra-virgin olive oil

1 hot or sweet Italian sausage, casing removed, crumbled

½ large or 1 small red or yellow bell pepper, thinly sliced

½ small red onion, or 1 medium shallot, thinly sliced (about ½ cup)

Handful of cherry tomatoes, halved

1 large garlic clove, thinly sliced

½ teaspoon kosher salt

¼ teaspoon dried oregano

⅛ teaspoon freshly ground black pepper

1 tablespoon red wine vinegar

½ (17-ounce) package shelf-stable gnocchi

¼ cup freshly and finely grated Parmigiano Reggiano cheese

1. Heat 1 tablespoon of the olive oil in a medium skillet over medium heat for 1 minute. Add a piece of sausage to the pan—if it sizzles immediately, the oil is hot enough; if not, wait until it does before adding the rest of the sausage. Cook, breaking up the sausage with a spoon and stirring so it cooks evenly, until browned and crisp, about 4 minutes. Use a slotted spoon to transfer the sausage to a plate, leaving any fat in the skillet.

2. Add the bell pepper and onion to the skillet and cook, stirring occasionally, until they start to soften, 2 to 3 minutes. Add the tomatoes, garlic, salt, oregano, and black pepper and stir to combine. Reduce the heat to medium-low, add 1 tablespoon water, and stir, scraping up any browned bits from the bottom of the pan. Cook, stirring occasionally, until the bell peppers have softened and the tomatoes have started to collapse, about 10 minutes. Stir in the vinegar and keep warm over the lowest heat possible.

3. Heat the remaining 1 tablespoon olive oil in a small nonstick skillet over medium-high heat for 1 minute. Add one of the gnocchi to the pan—if it sizzles immediately, the oil is hot enough; if not, wait until it does before adding the rest. Cook the gnocchi, stirring or tossing only every 2 minutes or so but otherwise resisting the urge to mess with them, until they are golden and crisp all over, 5 to 6 minutes total.

4. Return the pepper mixture to medium heat, add the crisp gnocchi and the sausage, and stir to combine. Transfer to a serving plate, top with the Parmesan, and serve.

Pasta Frittataatatata

"It's so cute and small"—something you will say about this frittata but shouldn't say to your boyfriend/husband/male-identifying slam piece (unless they're into that kinda thing). For fun, while cooking this, you should do what I did and pretend you're in the chorus of the musical *Chicago* and throw jazz hands up while you shout "FRITTATA!" with an a cappella hi-hat and a rhythmic, jazzy whisper. *"Ta, ta-ta ta . . . ta-ta, ta . . . FRITTATA!"*

Serves 1

½ teaspoon whole black peppercorns

3 large eggs

¼ cup freshly and finely grated Parmigiano Reggiano cheese

½ teaspoon kosher salt (use ¼ teaspoon if your pasta is well seasoned)

1 cup leftover cooked pasta, preferably spaghetti or a similar shape

¼ cup frozen peas

2 slices bacon, cut into bite-size pieces

1. Preheat the oven to 450°F.

2. Place the peppercorns in a small zip-top bag or a kitchen towel and bash them with a skillet until they're coarsely cracked. Transfer to a medium bowl and add the eggs, cheese, and salt. Whisk until no streaks of egg whites remain, then add the pasta and peas and stir to combine.

3. In a small (ideally nonstick) ovenproof skillet, cook the bacon over medium heat, undisturbed, until it starts sizzling, about 2 minutes, then cook for another minute before stirring. Cook, stirring very occasionally, until the bacon is golden and crisp, 3 to 5 minutes more. Use a slotted spoon to transfer the bacon to the egg mixture, leaving the fat in the skillet. Fold the bacon into the eggs.

4. Pour the egg mixture into the skillet, spreading it into an even layer. Cook until the edges start to set, about 30 seconds, then transfer the skillet to the oven. Bake for 6 to 7 minutes, until the center is just barely set (it will cook a little more as it rests). Transfer the frittata from the pan to the cutting board and let rest for 5 minutes before slicing and serving.

Rizzo-tto with Peas and Parm

The character Rizzo from *Grease* does not get the love she deserves. She was a strong, independent woman who was the leader of the coolest girl group in school. She was raised by her divorced single mom, and the jerks at school mocked her for getting pregnant. They were all just jealous virgins. What she overcame in that ridiculous movie was insurmountable, but she was resilient like Arborio rice. I firmly believe she would love this recipe, so this is for her. (Sushi rice works, too, if you happen to have it on hand; say, perhaps, for the rainbow rolls on page 65!). For reasons we don't need to get into, risotto is much easier to make for one than for many. And to settle the age-old debate of whether risotto is rice or pasta: Bruh, it's rice. When you want something filling and gooey but "need a vegetable," this totally counts.

Serves 1

- ¾ teaspoon kosher salt
- 1½ tablespoons unsalted butter
- 1 medium shallot, finely chopped
- ½ cup Arborio or sushi rice
- ¼ cup dry white wine (whatever you want to drink the rest of)
- ½ cup frozen peas (not thawed)
- ½ cup freshly and finely grated Parmigiano Reggiano cheese, plus more for serving
- ⅛ teaspoon freshly ground black pepper

1. In a small pot, combine 2½ cups water and ½ teaspoon of the salt and bring to a simmer over low heat.

2. Melt 1 tablespoon butter in a medium nonstick skillet over medium-low heat. Add the shallot and remaining ¼ teaspoon salt and cook, stirring almost continuously to prevent the shallot from getting any color, until soft but not browned, about 5 minutes. Add the rice and stir until the rice is translucent at the edges, about 3 minutes. Add the wine and cook, stirring, until it has nearly evaporated, 1 to 2 minutes.

3. Now comes the therapeutic part: While stirring continuously, add a ladleful (or ½ cup, if you don't have a ladle) of the simmering salty water. Cook, stirring, until the water has been absorbed, then add another ladleful and repeat, adjusting the heat as needed to keep the risotto bubbling gently and steadily, until you've added all the water and the rice is al dente and creamy, about 20 minutes.

4. Add the peas and cook until they're bright green, 1 to 2 minutes. Remove from the heat and stir in the Parmesan and remaining ½ tablespoon butter, then the pepper. Enjoy with more Parm on top.

Chicken Potpie

You ever seen a baby potpie? You're about to. I rarely dip my toe into the potpie game because it always felt like something an old person would eat and I, a young cool person, would never. But then I made this, and now I can declare that the youths are reclaiming potpie. I used an adorable mini pie dish I found in the baking aisle at a grocery store (if you ever see one, grab it—it'll come in handy for this and other recipes!).

Serves 1

- 1 tablespoon vegetable oil, such as canola
- 1 (5- to 6-ounce) boneless, skinless chicken thigh, or 3 chicken breast tenders (about 6 ounces total)
- ¼ teaspoon kosher salt, plus more as needed
- Freshly ground black pepper
- 1 tablespoon unsalted butter
- ½ small yellow onion, or 1 medium shallot, finely chopped (about ½ cup)
- 1 garlic clove, finely chopped
- 1 tablespoon all-purpose flour
- ¼ cup whole milk or heavy cream, plus more for brushing
- 1 teaspoon chicken bouillon paste (or use ½ cup chicken broth and skip the water)
- ⅛ teaspoon dried thyme or rosemary
- 1 disk store-bought pie dough, thawed if necessary but kept cold
- ½ cup frozen pea and carrot mix (or just frozen peas, if that's what you've got)

1. Preheat the oven to 400°F. You'll need either a 6-inch mini pie dish or a small (roughly 6½ × 5-inch) glass baking dish or metal baking pan.

2. Heat the oil in a small skillet over medium heat for 1 minute. Season the chicken with the salt and a pinch of pepper. Add the chicken to the pan and cook, undisturbed, until it's browned on the bottom and releases easily from the pan (if it sticks, it's not ready yet), about 3 minutes. Flip the chicken and cook until cooked through (if you cut into it, there should be no pink inside), 3 to 6 minutes more. Transfer the chicken to a plate to rest for 5 minutes, then shred or chop it.

3. In the same pan, melt the butter over medium-low heat. Add the onion and cook, stirring continuously to prevent any browning, until softened and translucent, about 3 minutes. Add the garlic and cook until fragrant, about 30 seconds. Sprinkle in the flour and cook, stirring and scraping the bottom of the pot continuously, until you can smell it toasting, about 1 minute.

4. Pour in ½ cup water and the milk, then add the bouillon paste and stir to break it up. Bring to a simmer and cook, stirring often to make sure nothing sticks to the bottom, until the mixture thickens slightly (it will thicken in the oven), 1 to 2 minutes. Stir in the thyme and remove from the heat.

5. Unroll the pie dough on your work surface and cut it into a rectangle that is 3 inches larger than the bottom of your baking dish (for a 6½ × 5-inch baking dish, that will be 9½ × 8 inches; if you have cut a slightly smaller rectangle than that or some of the corners are rounded, that's fine). Reserve the scraps! Gently drape the dough over the baking dish, easing it into the bottom corners and taking care to hold the edges gently so you don't tear the dough. Scatter the chicken in the crust, followed by the pea and carrot mix. Pour the sauce over the top.

Recipe continues

6. Gather up the dough scraps and roll them out into a ⅛-inch-thick rectangle slightly larger than the baking dish. Gently drape the dough over the baking dish and trim off all but ½ inch of the overhanging dough around the edges. Fold the overhanging dough in and under itself, then crimp it with your fingers or a fork. Refrigerate for 10 minutes to chill the dough.

7. Brush the top with milk to help the dough brown beautifully. Use a sharp knife to cut two 1-inch-long slits in the top to let steam escape and sprinkle with a pinch each of salt and pepper.

8. Place the baking dish on a small baking sheet to catch any drips. Bake for 60 to 70 minutes, until the crust is golden on the bottom (if you have a glass pie plate, you can check) and the filling is bubbling. Remove from the oven and let cool for 10 minutes before digging in.

Jollof Rice

Jollof rice is a West African rice dish full of herbs and spices mixed to make one mouthwatering meal. In the event you did zero research prior to buying this book, I am Black! And according to the spit I put in a tube and mailed to the unknown, my roots predominantly stem from Nigeria and Ghana, countries that both have their own version of jollof rice. Those roots go pretty far back, and since I grew up in a white suburb, I never saw no jollof rice, so now I'm making up for lost time. Like a fourth date with someone, this can be a side dish or a main, served with a protein like grilled chicken.

Serves 2 as a side or 1 as a main

1 small red bell pepper, coarsely chopped (about ¾ cup)

1 small plum tomato, coarsely chopped (about ½ cup)

1 small red onion, halved: ½ coarsely chopped (about ½ cup), ½ thinly sliced (about ½ cup)

1 garlic clove, peeled

1 (½-inch) piece fresh ginger, peeled and coarsely chopped

⅛ teaspoon cayenne pepper or other ground chile powder, or to taste

1 tablespoon extra-virgin olive oil

½ teaspoon kosher salt

½ teaspoon curry powder

¼ teaspoon freshly ground black pepper

⅛ teaspoon dried thyme

1 heaping teaspoon tomato paste

1 bay leaf

½ teaspoon chicken bouillon paste (or use ½ cup vegetable stock and skip the water)

½ cup basmati rice, rinsed

1. In a blender, combine the red bell pepper, tomato, chopped onion, garlic, ginger, and cayenne. Blend on high speed until smooth, 30 to 60 seconds. Transfer the mixture to a glass measuring cup; you should have about 1 cup. If you have way more than that, scoop some out to get down to 1 cup.

2. Heat the olive oil in a medium saucepan over medium heat for 1 minute. Add a piece of the sliced onion to the pan—if it sizzles immediately, the oil is hot enough; if not, wait a minute and try again. Add the remaining sliced onion, the salt, curry powder, black pepper, and thyme and cook, stirring continuously, until the onion has started to soften and the spices smell toasted, 1 to 2 minutes. Add the tomato paste and cook, stirring continuously, until it darkens but before it starts to scorch on the bottom of the pot, about 1 minute.

3. Add the pureed tomato mixture and the bay leaf and bring to a simmer. Adjust the heat if necessary so the mixture bubbles steadily and cook, stirring often and scraping the bottom, until the mixture reduces to ½ cup (keep that measuring cup close by so you can check your progress). The timing will depend on a lot of factors, but start checking around 10 minutes.

4. Add ½ cup water and the bouillon paste and stir to combine. Bring to a boil, then add the rice and stir. Cover the rice mixture with either a piece of parchment paper or aluminum foil directly on the surface to trap the steam, then cover the pot. Reduce the heat to low and cook for 20 minutes. Uncover and stir gently, then cover again with the parchment and lid and cook until the rice is tender, 10 to 15 minutes more.

Recipe continues

5. If you like the little burned bits at the bottom of the pot, uncover the pan and increase the heat to medium-high (if you don't want to crisp your rice, skip ahead to the steaming in step 6). Cook, turning the pot a quarter turn every 15 seconds, until you hear crackling on the bottom and smell just the tiniest hint of char (smoke), 1 to 2 minutes.

6. Remove the pan from the heat, cover with just the lid, and let the rice steam for 10 minutes. Uncover, remove the bay leaf, fluff the rice, and serve.

Savory Dutch Baby, Baby

I originally was only familiar with the sweet Dutch baby, a puffed, popover type of baked pancake. Back in Highland Park (and also a gift certificate prize in the original *Mean Girls* movie) the Walker Bros. Pancake House was where my high school friends and I debriefed our weekends over their silver dollar pancakes and giant Dutch babies. This felt like a fun twist for a nostalgic dish from my carb- and gossip-heavy adolescence. For best results, when you finish, announce the name of the dish like you're Austin Powers.

Serves 1

2 tablespoons unsalted butter

½ cup whole milk, at room temperature

½ cup all-purpose flour

2 large eggs, at room temperature

¼ teaspoon kosher salt

⅛ teaspoon freshly ground black pepper

4 tablespoons finely chopped fresh herbs, such as dill, chives, and/or parsley

Zest of ½ lemon

1 garlic clove, grated

For Serving

1 heaping spoonful of full-fat sour cream

1 or 2 pieces lox or smoked salmon

1 lemon wedge

1. Preheat the oven to 425°F. Place the butter in an 8-inch oven-safe skillet (cast-iron works best) and place the pan in the oven as it preheats.

2. In a blender, combine the milk, flour, eggs, salt, and pepper (or combine the ingredients in a tall mason jar or quart container and use an immersion blender). Carefully remove the skillet from the oven and pour about half the melted butter into the blender. Swirl the remaining butter around the skillet to coat the sides and return it to the oven. Blend on medium-high speed until smooth, just 10 seconds or so, making sure there aren't any clumps of flour. Stir 1 tablespoon of the herbs, the lemon zest, and the garlic into the batter.

3. Carefully pull out the oven rack with the skillet and pour in the batter. Bake (without opening the oven door!) for 13 to 18 minutes, until the edges of the pancake are golden and the center is puffed up.

4. Remove from the oven and serve the pancake hot, right from the pan. Dollop the sour cream in the center of the pancake and drape the lox next to it. Sprinkle the remaining 3 tablespoons herbs on top. Squeeze the juice from the lemon wedge over everything and eat immediately.

You Say Potato, I Say Galette

Panicked because you've got a great salad but need a little more substance? Well, there's no need to call the whole dinner thing off, because you can make a potato galette (pronounced like "mullet" with a *guh*). Composed of thinly sliced potatoes swimming in herbs and a creamy sauce hugged by a ring of dough, this is an excellent side dish that you can pretend is a well-balanced meal. This is a great time to use a mandoline if you've got one, and wear those gorgeous kitchen gloves you've been dying to take for a spin.

Serves 1

2 baby Yukon Gold potatoes (about 2 inches each)

2 teaspoons extra-virgin olive oil

Splash (call it 1 teaspoon) of dry white wine, such as Pinot Grigio (optional)

1 garlic clove, grated

½ teaspoon chopped fresh thyme leaves (from about 3 sprigs), or ½ teaspoon dried, plus more for serving

¼ teaspoon kosher salt

⅛ teaspoon freshly ground black pepper

¼ cup freshly grated Gruyère cheese

4 tablespoons freshly and finely grated Parmigiano Reggiano cheese

1 disk store-bought pie dough, thawed if necessary but kept cold

1 large egg

1. Slowly and carefully cut the potatoes into round slices as thin as you can manage, about ⅛ inch thick (use a mandoline if you have one). Place them in a medium bowl, add the olive oil, wine (if using), garlic, thyme, salt, and pepper, and toss everything to coat. Stir in the Gruyère and 2 tablespoons of the Parmesan.

2. Line a baking sheet with parchment paper. Unroll the pie dough and cut it into a 7-inch round. Transfer the dough to the prepared baking sheet. Arrange the sliced potatoes over the dough, leaving a 1-inch border all around and keeping the layer of potatoes as evenly thick as possible. Fold the exposed dough up and over the potatoes toward the center, pleating and pinching the dough as you go and leaving the potatoes at the center exposed. Refrigerate the galette for 15 to 20 minutes.

3. Meanwhile, preheat the oven to 400°F.

4. In a small bowl, whisk the egg until no streaks of egg white remain. Brush the dough with the egg wash, then sprinkle the dough and the exposed filling with the remaining 2 tablespoons Parmesan. Bake for 40 to 45 minutes, until the crust is golden brown and the potatoes are browned on top and tender all the way to the bottom when you poke them with a small, sharp knife. Remove from the oven and let the galette cool on the pan for at least 10 minutes or up to 1 hour before topping with thyme and serving.

Ride or Die Pad Thai

The ride-or-die—the person, or people, in your life that you'd do anything for. Some of mine are listed in the acknowledgments (unless I forgot them), and when we get together, we usually order Thai. It's one of the cuisines where we can find something we all like and that suits our annoying dietary restrictions and, better yet, that we can share. But forget those losers, you're cooking for one now! Pad thai has always been a comfort food for me, not only because it is one of the few things whose spice level won't kill me, but because it's an easy thing to toss together. The white vinegar is a trick from Kris Yenbamroong, who owns the fabulous restaurant Night + Market in LA.

Serves 1

4 ounces flat rice noodles

2 tablespoons palm sugar or light brown sugar

2 tablespoons fish sauce

2 tablespoons distilled white vinegar

1 tablespoon vegetable oil, such as canola

4 ounces large shrimp, peeled and deveined; 4 ounces extra-firm tofu, pressed (see page 167) and cut into bite-size pieces; or 1 (5- to 6-ounce) boneless, skinless chicken thigh, cut into thin strips

1 large egg, lightly beaten

Handful of bean sprouts

3 scallions, white and green parts cut into 2-inch lengths, and whites halved vertically

2 tablespoons finely chopped roasted peanuts

Roasted chile flakes or red pepper flakes, for serving (optional)

1 or 2 lime wedges, for serving

1. Place the noodles in a medium bowl, add enough hot tap water to cover them, and swish them around so they don't clump together. Let soak for 30 minutes, then drain.

2. Bring a small pot of water to a boil over high heat. Add the drained noodles and cook until they are tender; the timing will depend on the type of noodle, but start checking after 2 minutes. Drain the noodles and rinse them with cold water to stop the cooking.

3. Meanwhile, in a small bowl, whisk together the palm sugar, fish sauce, and vinegar until the sugar has dissolved.

4. Heat the oil in a large skillet over medium-high heat until you see faint wisps of smoke coming from the pan, a couple of minutes. Add the shrimp, spread them in a single layer, and cook, undisturbed, until they look cooked around the edges but still just a little uncooked in the center, about 1 minute (if you're using tofu or chicken, cook for 2 to 3 minutes; for tofu, you're just browning the bottom). Cook, stirring often, until the shrimp are totally opaque, 30 seconds more (or 1 to 2 minutes for tofu or chicken). Transfer the shrimp to a plate so they don't overcook (tofu or chicken can stay).

5. Add the drained noodles and the sauce to the pan and cook, stirring continuously, until the noodles are tender and have absorbed the sauce, about 1 minute. Push the noodle mixture to one side of the pan and pour the egg into the other. Cook the egg, stirring and scrambling continuously, until just barely set and dry, 30 seconds. Add the bean sprouts and scallions to the pan and quickly stir to mix everything together. Return the shrimp to the pan, if necessary.

6. Transfer the noodles to a plate, top with the roasted peanuts and some chile flakes, if you like, and serve right away, with the lime wedge alongside for squeezing.

Sizzled

& Crisp

Garlic Rosemary Pork Chop

The fancy dinner party for one continues. This was another recipe that I tested at 11 p.m. and only meant to have a bite of but ultimately finished off. We're not reinventing the wheel here, as garlic and rosemary are the hottest couple since Romeo and Juliet, who stand as a good reason to stay in and eat dinner alone instead of going to your mortal enemy's party.

Serves 1 or 2

1 tablespoon light brown sugar

1 tablespoon Dijon mustard

1½ teaspoons kosher salt

1 (1-inch-thick) bone-in pork chop

5 garlic cloves, smashed and peeled

3 sprigs rosemary

¼ teaspoon freshly ground black pepper

1 tablespoon vegetable oil, such as canola

2 tablespoons unsalted butter

1. In a small bowl, stir together ¼ cup water, the brown sugar, mustard, and 1 teaspoon salt until the sugar has dissolved. Place the pork chop in a quart-size zip-top bag, then add 3 garlic cloves and 2 rosemary sprigs. Pour in the marinade, press out all the air, and seal the bag, then lay it flat on a small baking sheet. Refrigerate for at least 1 hour or up to 24 hours, if you've got the time and patience.

2. When you're ready to cook, remove the pork from the refrigerator (but leave it in the marinade) and let it come to room temperature, 45 minutes to 1 hour. Remove the chop from the marinade and pat it dry, then season it all over with the remaining ½ teaspoon salt and the pepper.

3. Heat the oil in a medium skillet over medium-high heat until you see very faint wisps of smoke, 2 to 3 minutes. Add the chop to the skillet and cook, flipping regularly to ensure even browning, until the pork registers 135°F at its thickest part, about 10 minutes total. (If you don't have a thermometer, 10 to 11 minutes of cooking should get you there.)

4. Add the butter, the remaining 2 garlic cloves, and remaining rosemary sprig to the skillet. Hold the skillet at a slight angle and use a spoon to baste the pork chop continuously with the butter, until it's golden brown (145°F, if you've got a thermometer), 1 to 2 minutes.

5. Transfer the pork chop to a plate to rest for 5 minutes before serving.

"Can You Ever Just Be Whelmed" Individual Beef Wellington

Full disclosure: This will require some time and effort. Beef Wellington is an English dish where you wrap a giant beef tenderloin, along with some seasonings, in a big sheet of pastry like a Christmas present. This is a fancy-pants meal you'd make to impress someone's parents, but tonight you're impressing yourself. The recipe title comes from a thought-provoking question asked by Gabrielle Union's character in *10 Things I Hate About You*. She rightfully notes that one can be underwhelmed and overwhelmed, but asks if you can just be whelmed. The answer is yes: Neither overwhelming nor underwhelming, this beef is perfectly whelmed.

Serves 1

1 (4- to 5-ounce) filet mignon, 1½ inches thick (see Note page 116)

¼ teaspoon kosher salt, plus more as needed

¼ teaspoon freshly ground black pepper, plus more as needed

1 tablespoon vegetable oil, such as canola

½ small shallot, coarsely chopped

1 garlic clove, coarsely chopped

4 white button mushrooms, coarsely chopped

1 tablespoon booze (use whatever you have an open bottle of: red wine, brandy, sherry, or bourbon) or water

½ tablespoon unsalted butter

1 sheet of puff pastry (half a 19-ounce box), thawed if frozen but kept cold

2 teaspoons Dijon mustard, as needed

2 slices prosciutto (optional)

1 large egg

1. Season the filet mignon all over with the salt and pepper. Heat the oil in a small skillet over medium-high heat until you see very faint wisps of smoke, 2 to 3 minutes. Add the steak and cook, undisturbed, for 2 minutes, then carefully check the bottom. If it's golden, flip the steak; if not, let it go for another 30 seconds and check again. Cook until golden on the second side, 2 to 3 minutes more, then use tongs to hold the steak upright and sear the edges until golden all over. Transfer the steak to a plate and refrigerate until fully chilled, about 2 hours. Set the skillet (and any fat in it) aside.

2. In a mini food processor, combine the shallot and garlic and pulse until finely chopped (or finely chop them by hand). Add the mushrooms and pulse until everything is very finely chopped but not broken down into a paste.

3. Set the skillet you used for the steak over medium heat. Add the mushroom mixture (it's fine if the pan isn't fully heated yet) and a pinch each of salt and pepper. Cook, stirring often, until the mushrooms release their liquid, it cooks off, and they start to sizzle in the fat and brown on the edges, 5 to 8 minutes total. Carefully add the booze and stir, scraping up the browned bits from the bottom of the pan. Add the butter and stir to melt it, then cook until the mixture is soft and there's no liquid pooling in the pan, about 3 minutes. Transfer the mixture to a small bowl and refrigerate it until fully chilled, about 1 hour.

4. Cut a 7-inch square from the puff pastry (save what's left for a half batch of the croissants on page 190). Spread half the chilled mushroom mixture in the center of the pastry in a circle the size of your steak.

Recipe continues

5. Remove the steak from the refrigerator (it's important that it be cold, so keep it in the refrigerator up until this point—you want to bake it cold!). Spread a thin layer of the mustard all over the steak (you might not need all of it). Wrap it with 1 slice of the prosciutto (if using), then wrap the other slice perpendicular to the first. Place the steak in the center of the circle of mushroom mixture and top it with the remaining mushroom mixture. Bring two opposite corners of the puff pastry up and over the steak, pinching the corners to seal, then repeat with the two remaining corners. Pinch the edges to completely seal the pastry, so you have an "x" seam across the top.

6. Line a baking sheet with parchment paper. Place the Wellington on the baking sheet, seam-side up. Refrigerate for 30 minutes or freeze for 15 minutes to ensure the pastry is cold before baking.

7. Preheat the oven to 450°F.

8. In a small bowl, whisk the egg until no streaks of egg white remain. Brush the egg wash all over the top and sides of the pastry. Bake for 25 to 30 minutes, until the pastry is deeply golden brown and the meat is 120°F in the center. Remove from the oven and let the Wellington rest for 5 to 10 minutes before serving.

Note

If you can only find a steak thicker than 1½ inches, check the pastry after 25 minutes of baking and tent it with foil if necessary to prevent it from browning too much before the meat finishes cooking.

First Studio Apartment Steak Frites

There it was . . . my new apartment building, at the end of a classic palm-lined California street in Koreatown. In 2015, I'd gotten my dream job of assisting a TV writer (hi, Charlie!) and decided it was time to live on my own; a 500-square-foot studio was now where I called home. I spent hours researching layouts, how to decorate, how to maximize space, etc. It was my first time feeling like an adult. When people came over—and by "people," I mean one person, because it was a studio—everything they saw was something I had chosen, and I took great pride in that. Memories like that are what this book is about—celebrating the big moments in a small way. Steak frites are hella expensive at a restaurant and now you've got an entire apartment to pay for by yourself, so at-home frites are an ideal solution. The tricky part of this dish is the same as sex with your partner in your studio apartment: You want the steaks and frites to finish at the same time ☺

Serves 1

1 small russet potato, cut into ¼-inch-thick fries

1 (6- to 7-ounce) filet mignon, 1½ to 2 inches thick

2 tablespoons unsalted butter, at room temperature

1 small garlic clove, grated

¼ teaspoon dried rosemary

¾ teaspoon kosher salt, plus more as needed

3 tablespoons vegetable oil, such as canola

¼ teaspoon freshly ground black pepper

1. Place the potatoes in a medium bowl, add water to cover, and set aside to soak for 45 minutes to 1 hour.

2. Preheat the oven to 400°F. Pull the filet mignon out of the fridge and let it come to room temperature.

3. In a small bowl, combine the butter, garlic, rosemary, and a pinch of salt. Mix with a fork until the ingredients are evenly distributed, then form the butter into two "pats" (they don't have to be pretty; they're going to melt) and refrigerate them.

4. Drain the potatoes and thoroughly shake them to remove as much water as possible.

5. Turn your exhaust fan on and open all your kitchen windows, then heat a medium or large cast-iron skillet over medium-high heat until lightly smoking. Add 1 tablespoon of the oil and swirl the pan to coat it. Pat the steak dry all over and season with ¼ teaspoon of the salt and the pepper. Place the steak in the skillet and cook, undisturbed, for 2 minutes, then take a peek underneath. If it's beautifully browned and crisped on the bottom, flip it; if it's not, cook for another minute and check again. Cook, undisturbed, until browned on the second side, about 2 minutes, then use tongs to hold the steak upright and sear all the edges, 1 to 2 minutes total.

Recipe continues

6. Place one of your butter pats on the steak and transfer the skillet to the oven. Bake until an instant-read thermometer inserted into the center of the steak registers 120°F for rare, 130°F for medium-rare, or 140°F for medium. Start checking the temperature after 2 minutes, then every 60 seconds after that until the steak is cooked to your desired doneness, 3 to 6 minutes total. Transfer the steak to a plate and let it rest for 15 minutes, or until the fries are done.

7. Pat the potatoes dry with paper towels. Dry the bowl you used to soak them, then return the potatoes to the bowl and add the remaining 2 tablespoons oil and ½ teaspoon salt. Toss to coat. Lift them out of the bowl, letting any excess oil drip off, and place them on the rack in an air fryer (it's okay if they're in more than one layer). Air-fry at 375°F for 10 minutes, tossing the fries halfway through. Increase the temperature to 400°F and air-fry for 6 to 10 minutes more (or even longer if you like your fries extra crispy!), tossing every 2 minutes, until the fries are golden and crisp to your liking. (See Note for alternate cooking instructions.)

8. Serve everything as soon as the fries come out of the air fryer. Transfer the steak to a serving plate and put the remaining pat of garlic butter on top to slowly melt. Pile the fries next to the steak and dig in.

Note

If you don't have an air fryer, line a baking sheet with parchment paper. Toss the fries with the oil and salt as directed, then lay them out on the prepared baking sheet. Place the pan in the oven (you can do this at the same time as the steak) and bake for 10 minutes, just until lightly golden, then toss. After you've pulled the steak from the oven, increase the temperature to 450°F, return the fries to the oven, and bake for about 15 minutes, until they're golden and crisp to your liking.

Chicken Shawarma

Bits of marinated chicken stuffed into a flavorful pita—that's the shawarma life. Shawarma is a friendly relative of doner kebab and a popular Middle Eastern dish. Traditionally it could be made with mutton, but that might be hard to come by at your local Trader Joe's, so chicken will do just fine.

Serves 1

Chicken

2 tablespoons plain full-fat Greek yogurt

1 tablespoon extra-virgin olive oil

1 large garlic clove, grated

½ teaspoon kosher salt

½ teaspoon freshly ground black pepper

½ teaspoon ground cumin

½ teaspoon sweet paprika

½ teaspoon ground sumac, plus more for garnish

Pinch of cayenne pepper

Pinch of ground turmeric

Pinch of ground cinnamon

2 boneless, skinless chicken thighs (about 8 ounces total)

½ small yellow onion, or 1 large shallot, cut into wedges

Sandwich

1 pita or other flatbread

¼ cup plain full-fat Greek yogurt

1 tablespoon mayonnaise

1 lemon wedge

1 small garlic clove, grated

⅛ teaspoon kosher salt

Sliced pickles, sliced tomatoes, sliced cucumber, and/or any other fixings you like

1. **Start with the chicken:** In a small bowl, stir together the yogurt, olive oil, garlic, salt, black pepper, cumin, paprika, sumac, cayenne, turmeric, and cinnamon. Add the chicken and onion and toss to coat. Cover the bowl with plastic wrap and refrigerate for at least 1 hour or up to overnight.

2. Preheat the oven to 425°F. Line a baking sheet with parchment paper. Remove the chicken from the refrigerator and set it out to take some of the chill off while the oven heats.

3. Spread the chicken and onions over the prepared baking sheet and bake for 25 to 30 minutes, until the chicken is cooked through and browned and crispy in spots. Transfer the chicken to a cutting board and let it rest for 10 minutes. Throw away the parchment.

4. **Make the sandwich:** Put the pita on the baking sheet, then stick it in the oven (which can be off—it will still be hot) for 2 to 3 minutes, flipping it once, to warm the bread.

5. In a small bowl, whisk together the yogurt, mayonnaise, the juice from the lemon wedge, the garlic, and the salt until smooth. This is our cheater's white sauce.

6. Cut the chicken into thin strips and chop the onion. If using pita, cut off the top quarter and stuff the chicken inside, then drizzle the white sauce over and top with any other fixings you like. If using another type of flatbread, lay the chicken and onion in the center, drizzle the sauce over, add the toppings, and roll it up.

Mary Had a Little Pesto Lamb Chop

I was hesitant to include lamb in the book as it can be a *niche* meat, but then I thought of Mary in the nursery rhyme. We know Mary brought her lamb to school, but what happened after? Well, it was 1830 and times were tough, so I bet Mary was home alone and had that little lamb for dinner. Too bad she didn't have pesto. (Probably.) It may take a little extra prep, and lamb ain't cheap, so first read all the way to the end to ensure this comes out perfectly. To my favorite sock puppet, Lamb Chop, thank you for the sacrifice of your brethren. And now that I think about it, what a savage name to have given her.

Serves 1

Lamb

1 tablespoon plus ¼ teaspoon kosher salt

1 tablespoon sugar (optional)

3 single-rib lamb chops (about 8 ounces total)

¼ teaspoon freshly ground black pepper

Pesto

1 tablespoon pine nuts or coarsely chopped blanched almonds

1 small garlic clove, coarsely chopped

⅛ teaspoon kosher salt

½ cup packed fresh basil leaves

2 tablespoons extra-virgin olive oil, plus more if needed

¼ cup freshly and finely grated Parmigiano Reggiano cheese

1 tablespoon vegetable oil, such as canola

1. **Make the lamb:** This step is optional but highly recommended if you think some lamb tastes too "lamby": In a medium bowl, combine 2 cups water, 1 tablespoon salt, and the sugar and stir until the salt and sugar have dissolved. Add the lamb chops, cover the bowl, and refrigerate for 24 hours, then rinse the lamb chops and pat them dry.

2. Season the lamb all over with the salt and pepper. Let it come to room temperature for about 30 minutes.

3. **Meanwhile, make the pesto:** In a medium or large cast-iron skillet, toast the pine nuts over medium-low heat, shaking the pan often, until golden, about 5 minutes. Transfer them to a mini food processor or blender and pulse until finely ground. Add the garlic and salt and pulse until the garlic is finely chopped. Add the basil and olive oil and process, stopping to scrape down the sides if you need to, until the pesto is well combined and as smooth as you like, just a few seconds. Add the Parmesan and pulse to combine. If the pesto is too thick for your liking, stir in more olive oil 1 teaspoon at a time.

4. In the skillet you used for the pine nuts, heat the vegetable oil over medium-high heat until you see very faint wisps of smoke, about 5 minutes. Add the lamb chops and cook, undisturbed, for 2 minutes, then carefully check one. If the bottom is golden and crisp, flip the chops; if not, cook them for 30 seconds more and check again. Cook until golden and crisp on the second side, 2 to 3 minutes more for a medium-rare chop (130°F in the thickest part). If you like your lamb medium (140°F), cook for another 30 seconds on each side. Transfer the lamb to a plate and let it rest for 5 minutes.

5. Spoon the pesto on a serving plate and top with the lamb chops and serve.

California Dreamin' Carnitas Tacos

Most people move to Los Angeles to pursue their dream of making it in Hollywood. A few others moved for the tacos. LA has some of the best tacos in the world (fight me), and I couldn't live with myself if some tacos didn't make their way into this book. Tacos are the perfect single-serving recipe because you can control how much goes into your taco, so you can have one taco with a buttload of carnitas or six tacos with just some carnitas. Now that's California dreamin'. This carnitas technique is inspired by Diana Kennedy's and involves basically simmering fatty pork shoulder in water for a couple of hours. In step 1, the meat will cook through and all the fat will render and end up pooling in the skillet. Keep cooking, and the meat will shred and crisp in the rendered fat. Spoon the delicious meat into warmed tortillas and top with cilantro, onion, and lime.

Serves 2, with leftovers

1 pound boneless pork shoulder steaks

1 small white onion, halved: ½ left whole, ½ finely chopped

1 dried bay leaf

1 teaspoon kosher salt

3 or 4 (4- to 6-inch) corn tortillas, warmed

½ cup finely chopped fresh cilantro leaves

1 lime, quartered

1. Slice the pork steaks against the grain into pieces about 1 inch thick. Place the pork in a medium skillet along with the onion half (just throw it in there!), the bay leaf, and the salt. Add just enough water to cover the meat. Bring to a boil over high heat, then reduce the heat to medium-low and simmer gently until all the water has evaporated and the meat is cooked through and tender. How long this takes will depend on a lot of factors, so just keep going until the water is gone and the meat is cooked! Could be 60 minutes, could be up to 90. If the water has evaporated before the meat is cooked, add a splash more water.

2. Keep cooking until the pork crisps in its own fat, stirring occasionally so that all sides brown without burning and adjusting the heat if it starts to get too browned, about another hour. As the meat softens, use two forks to shred it into bits and stir so all the pork gets crispy. Remove the bay leaf and onion.

3. Serve the carnitas in the warmed tortillas, topped with the chopped onion, the cilantro, and a squeeze of lime juice.

Note

If you are like me and don't looooove touching meat, ask the butcher if they'll do this for you. If you can't find pork shoulder steaks (which are thinly sliced pork shoulder), pick out the smallest pork shoulder, remove the bone (if it's still there), and cut a pound of it into 1-inch cubes to make carnitas. Slice the extra shoulder into 1-inch steaks and freeze them for the future. They're like what you always wanted from a pork chop—juicy, fatty, greasy—without the risk of toughness. Grill or sear them over medium-high heat for 3 to 5 minutes per side.

Tryna Smash Smashburger Sliders

Back in college when girls in my sorority were on the hunt for new paramours, we'd always ask if they were "tryna." There was no need to ask what, specifically, they were trying to do—that was implied. They were trying to smash, which meant fornicate. Why a smashburger? In this context, it's not a weird sex term. I find that too thick a burger creates a lot of mouth work, and this book is about simplicity. You're getting two thin sliders that are enough to fuel social fornication endeavors. Godspeed, horndog.

Makes 2 sliders

- ½ medium shallot, thinly sliced into rings
- 4 ounces ground beef, ideally 80/20
- 1 teaspoon Worcestershire sauce
- ¼ teaspoon garlic powder
- ¼ teaspoon kosher salt
- ⅛ teaspoon freshly ground black pepper
- 1 tablespoon unsalted butter
- 2 Hawaiian rolls or other small rolls, split
- 1 slice cheddar or American cheese, cut into quarters (optional)
- ½ small plum tomato, very thinly sliced crosswise
- 1 large romaine lettuce leaf, rib removed, torn into quarters
- Ketchup, mustard, mayo, or other burger condiment of your choosing

1. Fill a small bowl with ice and water and add the shallot rings. Let them soak and mellow until you're ready to serve. Cut 8 small squares of parchment paper.

2. In a medium bowl, use clean hands to mix the ground beef, Worcestershire, garlic powder, salt, and pepper just until well combined (don't mix any more than that or you'll have a tough burger). Divide the mixture into 4 portions and roll each into a ball. Sandwich each ball between 2 squares of parchment. Use a cast-iron skillet or other heavy pan to press down on one burger at a time until it's very thin and about 4 inches across.

3. Melt the butter in a medium or large cast-iron skillet over medium heat. Add the rolls, cut-side down, and cook until golden on the bottom, 2 to 3 minutes. Transfer to a plate.

4. Increase the heat to medium-high. When the pan is lightly smoking, peel the top layer of parchment off one of the burgers and place the burger in the hot pan, exposed-side down. Firmly press the burger into the hot pan with your spatula, then peel back the other layer of parchment. Repeat with all the burgers. Cook until the bottom sides are very crisp and deeply browned, about 2 minutes. Flip, cook for 1 minute, then add a slice of cheese (if using) to each burger and cover the pan. Cook until the cheese has melted and the bottoms of the burgers are crisped, another 1 minute. Spread your condiment of choice on the bottom of the bun and top with lettuce. Stack two patties on top.

5. Drain the shallots and pat them dry with paper towels. Top each burger with shallots and a tomato slice or two. Add the top buns and close the burgers. Eat right away!

Air Fryer Coconut Shrimp

Coconut shrimp is one of my favorite appetizers to get at a restaurant but not something you might think to make at home. Unless you're me, because I'm always craving coconut shrimp. Wish I could have it right now. Using an air fryer minimizes mess and cuts down on cook time. The shrimp is sprayed with an oil spray to get it crispy, so I'd recommend going coco-nuts and buying coconut oil spray to enhance the flavor.

Serves 1

- 1/3 cup sweetened shredded coconut
- 1/3 cup panko breadcrumbs
- Coconut oil spray or avocado oil spray
- 2 large eggs
- 1/4 cup cornstarch
- 1/2 teaspoon kosher salt
- 1/8 teaspoon garlic powder
- 1/8 teaspoon freshly ground black pepper
- Pinch of cayenne pepper (optional)
- 8 ounces large shrimp (21/25 count), thawed if frozen, peeled, and deveined
- 1/2 lime
- Flaky salt, for garnish
- Sweet chili sauce, for serving

1. Line your air fryer basket with aluminum foil. Add the coconut and breadcrumbs and spray twice with oil to lightly coat. Air-fry at 375°F for 1 minute, then check. If the mixture is toasted and golden, pull it from the air fryer; if not, air-fry for another 30 seconds and check again. Set the breading aside.

2. Crack the eggs in a small shallow bowl and whisk with a fork until no streaks of egg white remain. In another small shallow bowl, stir together the cornstarch and half the salt to combine. In a third small shallow bowl, combine the toasted coconut and breadcrumbs, the remaining salt, the garlic powder, black pepper, and cayenne (if using) and toss to mix.

3. Pat the shrimp dry. Working with one at a time, coat the shrimp in the seasoned cornstarch and shake off any excess. Dip the shrimp into the egg and let the excess drip off. Finally, put the shrimp into the coconut mixture and toss to coat, then press lightly to make sure the shrimp is evenly breaded all over. Place the breaded shrimp on a plate and repeat with the remaining shrimp.

4. Remove and discard the foil from the air fryer basket. Place the shrimp in the basket in a single layer (work in batches if they don't all fit) and spray the tops generously with oil. Air-fry at 375°F for 2 minutes. Flip all the shrimp and spray the other side evenly with oil. Air-fry for 2 minutes more, or until the shrimp are cooked through, golden, and crispy. If they aren't firm and are still translucent in the middle, cook for 30 seconds more and check again; repeat as needed until the shrimp are opaque and cooked through.

5. Transfer the shrimp to a plate, generously squeeze the juice from the lime half over, then sprinkle with a bit of flaky salt. Enjoy immediately with the sweet chili sauce in a small bowl alongside for dipping.

Note

If you don't have an air fryer, preheat the oven to 375°F. Spread the coconut and breadcrumbs on a baking sheet and spray twice with oil. Bake for 3 to 5 minutes, until golden brown. Proceed with the breading directions, then bake the shrimp for 8 to 9 minutes, flipping them after 5 minutes, until golden, crispy, and cooked through.

Rice for One

Makes about 1½ cups

½ cup jasmine or other long-grain white rice

Kosher salt

Place the rice in a small bowl and add cold water to cover. Swish it around gently with your hand, then pour off the water. Repeat two or three times until the water runs clear, then transfer the drained rice to a small saucepan and add ¾ cup water and a pinch of salt. Wrap the lid of the pot in aluminum foil to prevent any steam from escaping. Bring the water to a gentle boil over medium heat, then reduce the heat to low, cover, and cook for 12 minutes. Remove from the heat and let the rice steam, still covered, for 10 minutes. Uncover and fluff the rice with a fork before serving.

Teriyaki Salmon

Easy and quick, like going to the DMV, this is an ideal meal for the busy individual on the go in need of some protein and omega-3 fatty acids. It's baller to be making teriyaki sauce from scratch, and you will lick the plate when you're done. I repeat: You *will* lick the plate when you're done. Serve this with some steamed broccoli and rice, and you've got a hot, healthy, well-balanced meal.

Serves 1

1 (6-ounce) skin-on salmon fillet, about 1 inch thick throughout

1/8 teaspoon kosher salt

1/8 teaspoon freshly ground black pepper

2 tablespoons soy sauce

1 tablespoon sake, dry sherry, rice wine, or water

1 tablespoon mirin

1 tablespoon light brown sugar

1 tablespoon vegetable oil, such as canola

1 scallion, green part only, thinly sliced

1/4 teaspoon sesame seeds, toasted

Rice for One (recipe on page 130) or 1 cup cooked white rice, for serving

1. Pull the salmon out of the fridge and let it come to room temperature. Pat the salmon dry all over with a paper towel. Season with the salt and pepper.

2. In a small bowl, whisk together the soy sauce, sake, mirin, and brown sugar until the sugar has dissolved.

3. Heat the oil in a medium skillet over medium heat for 1 minute. Add a piece of scallion to the pan—if it sizzles immediately, the oil is hot enough; if not, wait until it sizzles rapidly. Remove the sacrificial scallion, then add the salmon to the pan, skin-side down, and press it gently with your spatula to encourage all the skin to come in contact with the pan. Cook, pressing gently in spots if needed to ensure the skin is touching the pan, for 4 minutes, then peek at the skin; if it's golden and crispy, flip the salmon skin-side up. If not, cook for another 30 seconds and check again before flipping. Cook until the salmon is just barely opaque all the way up the sides, 1 to 3 minutes more.

4. Remove the pan from the heat and carefully pour in the sauce—it will splatter a lot! Return the pan to medium heat and cook, continuously spooning the sauce over the salmon, until the sauce has reduced and looks glazy and the salmon is cooked to your liking (if the salmon flakes easily with a fork, it's cooked), 1 to 2 minutes for medium, or 3 to 4 minutes for medium-well. If your salmon is done before the sauce reduces, transfer it to a plate and continue to reduce the sauce.

5. Transfer the salmon to a plate with the crispy skin facing up (you can remove the skin, though it's very tasty) and drizzle with as much of the sauce as you like. Sprinkle with the scallion and sesame seeds and serve with rice.

Air Fryer Fish Tacos

People moved to Los Angeles for their Hollywood dreams and tacos. I would be remiss (and banned from the state) if I didn't bring up *fish tacos,* which deserve their own star on the Walk of Fame. With fish battered and air-fried to minimize grease, these tacos are a quick and easy way to satisfy your seafood cravings—no need to brave the 405, the PCH, or the 10 just to get to the ocean.

Serves 2 (makes 4 tacos)

Lime Crema

2 tablespoons full-fat sour cream or mayonnaise, or a mix

Pinch of chipotle chile powder

Pinch of kosher salt plus more if needed

1 lime, cut into wedges plus more if needed

Fish

⅓ cup plus 2 tablespoons all-purpose flour

⅓ cup cornstarch

1 teaspoon kosher salt

½ teaspoon ground cumin

½ teaspoon garlic powder

¼ teaspoon chipotle chile powder

1 (12-ounce) can of beer, ideally Mexican lager

2 tablespoons vegetable oil, such as canola

1 (4- to 5-ounce) tilapia fillet, thawed if frozen

Nonstick cooking spray

Tacos

8 small soft corn tortillas, warmed

1 cup shredded green cabbage or bagged slaw mix

2 tablespoons crumbled Cotija cheese (optional)

1 tablespoon fresh cilantro leaves

1 small radish, thinly sliced

Hot sauce, for serving

1. **Make the lime crema:** In a small bowl, combine the sour cream, chile powder, and salt and squeeze in the juice from 1 lime wedge. Stir until thoroughly combined, then taste and add the juice from another lime wedge and/or more chipotle powder, if you like. It should be drizzle-able, so add water 1 teaspoon at a time if it's too thick.

2. **Fry the fish:** Line the basket of your air fryer with aluminum foil if it's perforated (if it's solid and nonstick, no need). In a shallow dish long enough to fit the fish, stir together ⅓ cup of the flour, the cornstarch, salt, cumin, garlic powder, and chile powder. Measure out ⅓ cup of the beer (save the rest to drink) and pour it into the dry mix along with the vegetable oil. Whisk until smooth. The batter should be very thick and there will be a lot of it, but we need to make sure we can thoroughly coat the fish.

3. Place the remaining 2 tablespoons flour on a plate and coat the fish in the flour, then shake off any excess. Submerge the fish in the batter and turn to coat evenly and completely.

4. Preheat the air fryer to 400°F (if that's not an option, run it for 1 minute at the same temperature). Coat the foil or air fryer basket generously with nonstick spray. Lift the fish out of the batter and transfer it to the air fryer basket. Air-fry for 8 to 9 minutes, until the batter on top is set and the fish lifts easily from the basket. Flip the fish and cook for 2 to 3 minutes more, until the crust is set and the edges are crispy. The fish will definitely be cooked through!

5. **Make the tacos:** Lay the tortillas on a serving plate, stacking two tortillas for each taco. Break the fish up into smaller chunks to fit in the tortillas. Divide the fish between them, then sprinkle over the cabbage, Cotija (if using), cilantro, and radish. Drizzle with the crema, add a few shakes of hot sauce, and dig in.

Lobstah Tail

The first time I ever had lobster was from a food truck. Mind you, it was from a famous, reputable food truck in LA. It was love at first dribble of butter down my chin (I am team #hotbutter over #coldmayo). I considered adding a lobster roll to the book, but it's much simpler to cook a single lobster tail and still get your luxurious crustacean fix. Make this when something worth celebrating happens—perhaps a relative you hate died and left you money. Or you found a pot of gold. Or got hired at a job that pays you more. Or seduced a sugar parent. Make this for any of those reasons, because fair warning, lobster ain't cheap.

Serves 1

1½ tablespoons unsalted butter, melted

1 garlic clove, grated

¼ teaspoon kosher salt

Pinch of cayenne pepper or freshly ground black pepper

1 lemon

1 (5- to 6-ounce) lobster tail, thawed if frozen (see Note)

4 fresh chives, thinly sliced (optional, but recommended)

1. Position a rack 6 inches from the broiler heating element and preheat the broiler to high. Line a small baking sheet with aluminum foil.

2. In a small bowl, combine the melted butter, garlic, salt, and cayenne. Grate a little bit of lemon zest into the bowl; use a Microplane grater and run the lemon over it just twice. Mix all the ingredients together.

3. Place the lobster tail on a cutting board, shell facing up. Use heavy kitchen scissors to cut the shell through the top, lengthwise through the middle, starting at the thicker end and cutting until you reach the fins. Flip the lobster tail over and cut through the underside of the shell lengthwise through the middle until you reach the fins again, so now the shell is cut in half, but the meat and fins are still intact. At this point, you can switch to a sharp knife or keep using the scissors: Cut lengthwise through the middle of the meat and the fins, so the tail is fully halved and the halves are separated. Thoroughly pat the lobster meat and shell dry.

4. Lay the two halves on the baking sheet, meat-side up. Drizzle a generous layer of the butter mixture over the exposed meat—save about half the butter in a small bowl for serving.

5. Broil the lobster for 4 to 6 minutes, until the meat is white and opaque and is firm but not stiff to the touch; check it often, as every broiler is different. (If you like to take the temperature, make sure the meat closest to the shell is 135°F.) If you like, pour any lobstery melted butter from the baking sheet into the small bowl with the remaining butter (or just dip in the straight butter). Garnish generously with the chives, if you're using them, and get dipping!

Note

Most lobster tails are sold frozen, and they'll need to be completely thawed before cooking or they may cook unevenly. Let the tail thaw in the refrigerator for 24 hours or put it in a plastic bag and submerge in cold water at room temperature for 1 to 2 hours.

Glazy &

Saucy

BBQ Salmon

Easing you into the chapter with our good friend salmon. Who says BBQ is for a crowd? From fridge to plate in less than 20 minutes, this is a healthy but saucy recipe to kick off your workweek. Simple enough for a Monday, special enough for a Friday.

Serves 1

Nonstick cooking spray

1 (6-ounce) salmon fillet, about 1 inch thick throughout

2 teaspoons vegetable oil, such as canola

¼ teaspoon kosher salt

⅛ teaspoon freshly ground black pepper

2 tablespoons of your favorite barbecue sauce, store-bought or homemade

1 teaspoon light brown sugar

Pinch of smoked paprika

Side salad of choice, for serving

1. Preheat the oven to 450°F. Position a rack 6 inches away from the broiler heating element. Line a small baking sheet with aluminum foil, then coat the foil with nonstick spray.

2. Pat the salmon dry with paper towels. Place it on the prepared baking sheet and coat it all over with the vegetable oil, then season with the salt and pepper. Brush the top and sides of the salmon with the barbecue sauce, then sprinkle the brown sugar and paprika on top.

3. Bake for 10 to 12 minutes for medium, or about 15 minutes for well-done, then check to see if the salmon flakes easily with a fork. Switch the oven to broil and broil for 1 to 2 minutes, until the sauce is bubbling. Serve right away alongside a simple salad.

BBQ Sauce

Makes ⅓ cup

¼ cup ketchup

1 tablespoon apple cider vinegar

2 teaspoons Worcestershire sauce

½ teaspoon onion powder or garlic powder

¼ teaspoon smoked paprika

Pinch of cayenne pepper

In a small saucepan, stir together the ketchup, vinegar, Worcestershire, onion powder, paprika, and cayenne. Bring to a simmer over medium heat, then cook, stirring occasionally, until slightly reduced and thickened, 5 to 8 minutes. Remove from the heat and let cool.

Wind Beneath Your Orange-Ginger Chicken Wings

I was my eighth-grade class president, which meant I got to pick the song the class sang at graduation. No one said no when I suggested "Because You Loved Me" by Celine Fucking Dion. Do you think a bunch of fourteen-year-olds can successfully hit that F5 with control in the climatic final chorus? Hell no. It was terrible. I will only admit this now, but the song I thought I had suggested was actually Bette Midler's "Wind Beneath My Wings," which is also a power ballad about gratitude and emotional support sung by an iconic woman. So, we sang the wrong song because I'm an idiot. I'm smarter now, and that's why for the individual servings, I opted to do drumettes and flats rather than a big old chicken breast. The zangy, tangy, citrusy sauce gives the wings just enough air to fly right into your mouth.

Serves 1

- Nonstick cooking spray
- 8 mixed pieces chicken wing drumettes and flats (about 12 ounces total)
- 1½ teaspoons baking powder
- ½ teaspoon kosher salt
- ¼ teaspoon freshly ground black pepper
- 1 teaspoon cornstarch
- 1 teaspoon vegetable oil, such as canola
- ¼ teaspoon red pepper flakes
- 1 (1-inch) piece fresh ginger, peeled and cut into thin matchsticks
- 1 garlic clove, minced
- 2 large strips of orange zest (removed with a vegetable peeler)
- 3 tablespoons fresh orange juice
- 2 tablespoons light brown sugar
- 1 tablespoon rice vinegar
- 1 tablespoon soy sauce
- ½ teaspoon sesame seeds, toasted

1. Preheat the oven to 425°F. Line a baking sheet with aluminum foil and set a wire rack on top. Coat the rack with nonstick spray.

2. In a large bowl, toss the chicken wings with the baking powder, salt, and pepper until they're evenly coated. Spread them out on the prepared rack. Bake for 45 to 55 minutes, turning them after 25 minutes, until they're browned and crispy all over.

3. **When the wings have about 10 minutes left, make the sauce:** In a small bowl, mix the cornstarch and 1 teaspoon cold water together until there are no lumps.

4. Heat the vegetable oil in a small skillet over medium heat for a couple of minutes. Add a pinch of red pepper flakes to the pan—if they sizzle immediately, the oil is hot enough; if not, wait a minute and try again. Add all the pepper flakes, the ginger, garlic, and orange zest. Cook, stirring continuously, until fragrant, just a few seconds. Add the orange juice, brown sugar, vinegar, and soy sauce and cook, stirring continuously, until the sugar has dissolved, just 30 seconds. Pour in the cornstarch mixture and keep stirring until the sauce is thick, another 30 seconds. Remove the pan from the heat immediately and, if the wings aren't ready yet, pour it into a small bowl.

5. Transfer the wings to a large bowl. Remove the orange zest from the sauce, then pour the sauce over the wings and toss to coat. Transfer to a serving plate, sprinkle with the sesame seeds, and dig in.

BBQ Pulled Chicken Sandwich

A 40-hour-a-week unpaid internship is what first brought me to LA in June 2010, but picking up two low-paid weekend jobs is what allowed me to stay that summer. One job was at a now-defunct pizza place in West Hollywood and the other was at a now-defunct BBQ food truck, which is where my love for sauced pulled meats developed. Sandwiches are easy to make a single serving of, but to get pulled chicken right, you need the proper measurements, which we certainly have. Yeehaw and giddyup.

Serves 1

BBQ Pulled Chicken

1 (5- to 6-ounce) boneless, skinless chicken thigh, or 2 chicken breast tenders

¼ teaspoon kosher salt, plus more as needed

Pinch of freshly ground black pepper

1 teaspoon vegetable oil, such as canola

Coleslaw

1 tablespoon mayonnaise, plus more as needed

1 teaspoon brine from your favorite jar of dill pickles

1 cup loosely packed very thinly shredded cabbage or bagged coleslaw mix

For Serving

1 hamburger bun, split

3 to 4 tablespoons of your favorite barbecue sauce, store-bought or homemade (page 139), as needed

3 dashes of Worcestershire sauce

Pinch of smoked paprika

4 dill pickle slices

1. **Make the chicken:** Season the chicken with the salt and pepper.

2. Heat the oil in a small skillet over medium heat for a minute. Add the chicken (we're not going for a ton of browning here, so it's okay if the pan isn't totally heated) and cook, flipping often so it doesn't get too browned, until it is cooked through (there should be no pink inside), 6 to 8 minutes. Transfer the chicken to a plate to rest for 5 minutes and keep the pan close by.

3. **Meanwhile, make the coleslaw:** In a small bowl, whisk together the mayonnaise, pickle brine, and a small pinch of salt. Add the cabbage and toss to coat, pressing or squeezing the cabbage as you work to help soften it. Let it sit for 5 to 10 minutes.

4. Use two forks to shred the chicken, making sure it's really pulled apart and there aren't any large pieces.

5. Spread both cut sides of the hamburger bun with a thin layer of mayonnaise. Return the small skillet to medium heat. Add the hamburger bun, cut-side down, and toast until it's lightly browned, 1 to 2 minutes, then transfer it to a plate. Add the shredded chicken, 3 tablespoons of the barbecue sauce, the Worcestershire, and the paprika to the skillet. If the chicken looks dry, add an additional tablespoon of barbecue sauce. Cook, stirring often, until the sauce is bubbling and has thickened slightly, 1 to 2 minutes.

6. Pile the chicken on the bottom of the bun, and top with the coleslaw and the pickles. Close the bun and serve right away.

She's Piccata Have It (Chicken)

Nola Darling, the protagonist of Spike Lee's 1986 film *She's Gotta Have It,* refuses to commit to any of the men she's dating and she would absolutely make this dish. Chicken piccata is a classic Italian dish with a wine-y, lemony, caper-y flavor. Which makes sense, since it contains wine, lemon, and capers. For the ignorant, a caper in this sense is not a heist film where criminals plan and execute a complex robbery, but rather the pea-size buds of a prickly flower that taste like a lemon and an olive had a baby.

Serves 1

1 boneless, skinless chicken breast (about 10 ounces)

¼ teaspoon kosher salt

¼ teaspoon freshly ground black pepper

¼ cup all-purpose flour

2 tablespoons extra-virgin olive oil

¼ cup white wine

2 garlic cloves, thinly sliced

1 tablespoon brined capers, plus a splash of their brine

Zest and juice of ½ lemon

1 tablespoon unsalted butter

2 teaspoons finely chopped fresh flat-leaf parsley, for serving

1. Place the chicken breast on a cutting board and hold it in place with the palm of your nondominant hand. Use a sharp knife to cut parallel to the cutting board so you cut the chicken into two thin cutlets. Freeze one of the cutlets for the next time a piccata craving strikes. Cover the other piece of chicken with plastic wrap and use a rolling pin or the bottom of a heavy skillet to pound it to an even ¼-inch thickness. Season the chicken all over with the salt and pepper.

2. Place the flour on a plate and spread it into a thin layer. Press the chicken into the flour, flip, and repeat to make sure it's coated all over, then gently shake off any excess flour so your chicken isn't gummy.

3. Heat the olive oil in a medium skillet over medium heat for 1 minute. Add a pinch of flour to the oil—if it sizzles immediately, it's hot enough; if not, wait another minute and try again. Add the chicken to the skillet and cook, undisturbed, until the chicken comes off the pan easily and is golden on the bottom, 3 to 4 minutes. Flip the chicken and cook until golden on the second side and cooked through, 2 to 3 minutes more. Transfer the chicken to a plate.

4. Remove the skillet from the heat and pour in the wine. Scrape up all the browned bits from the bottom of the pan. Return the pan to medium heat, add the garlic, capers, and caper brine, and cook, stirring continuously, until the garlic has softened, about 1 minute. Add the lemon zest and juice, then add the butter and swirl the pan until it melts. Return the chicken to the pan and cook, swirling the pan to help the sauce emulsify, until it's thick and creamy, about 1 minute.

5. Transfer the chicken to a serving plate and pour the sauce over, then sprinkle with the parsley and serve right away.

This Little Piggy Became Pork Marbella Meatballs

I've always been amused by how different those ten little piggies were. One got to go to the market, one chilled at home, one had high cholesterol from all the roast beef, the other was a simpleton who wanted for nothing, and one was a crybaby. Living under the same roof as all those piggies would make me move out ASAP and host a permanent party for one. I digress . . . pork marbella is usually made with a full tenderloin, but that's simply too much food so we're converting them to manageable meatballs. There's a lot of flavor in this dish and it will leave this little piggy saying, "Wow, my friends taste good!" This recipe calls for an ovenproof skillet, but ideally not one made of cast iron, which can react with the acidic ingredients and add an unwanted metallic flavor, unless you're into that kinda thing.

Serves 2

- 1 large egg
- 3 tablespoons panko breadcrumbs
- ½ teaspoon kosher salt
- 1¼ teaspoons dried oregano
- ⅛ teaspoon freshly ground black pepper
- 8 ounces ground pork (preferably not lean)
- 1 tablespoon extra-virgin olive oil
- ½ cup dry white wine
- ¼ cup pitted green olives, such as Castelvetrano (about 10 olives)
- 4 pitted prunes, halved
- 2 tablespoons red wine vinegar
- 2 tablespoons light brown sugar
- 1 tablespoon brined capers, plus a splash of their brine
- 2 garlic cloves, smashed and peeled
- 1 bay leaf
- 1 tablespoon fresh flat-leaf parsley, for serving

1. Preheat the oven to 350°F.

2. In a medium bowl, combine the egg, breadcrumbs, salt, ¼ teaspoon of the oregano, and the pepper with a fork. Add the pork and mix with your hands until thoroughly and evenly combined (but no more than that or the mixture will be tough). Divide the mixture into 4 hefty meatballs.

3. Heat a small nonreactive ovenproof skillet over medium-high heat. When the pan is hot, add the olive oil, then the meatballs, and cook, undisturbed, until deep golden brown on the bottom, 2 to 3 minutes. Turn the meatballs a quarter turn and cook until deep golden brown on the second side, 2 to 3 minutes more. Remove the skillet from the heat.

4. Add the wine, olives, prunes, vinegar, brown sugar, capers and their brine, garlic, remaining 1 teaspoon oregano, and the bay leaf. Stir everything together, swishing the meatballs around in the mixture to coat. Return the pan to medium heat and bring to a simmer, turning the meatballs so one of the uncooked sides is facing up.

5. As soon as the sauce simmers, transfer the skillet to the oven and bake for 15 minutes. Switch the oven to broil (on high, if that's an option) and broil for about 5 minutes—but check regularly as every broiler is different—until the sauce is syrupy and the meatballs are browned and cooked through (a thermometer inserted into the center should read 165°F, or you can sacrifice a meatball to make sure there's no pink inside).

6. Remove the bay leaf, sprinkle with the parsley, and serve right away.

“No First Date” Ribs

Do not order ribs on a first date. I made that mistake when I went out to eat at a barbecue restaurant with a man I thought I'd marry. I'd been craving ribs, as one does, so I ordered them. I remember the ribs being excellent, which means I absolutely had sauce on my face and ate them like a feral beast. I did not get asked on a second date. Lesson learned: Ribs are meant to be eaten in the company of close friends or alone at home. You think you need a crowd to make ribs, but in fact one rack of baby back ribs is only about ten ribs, which I'd say is about two meals, making this an easy recipe to satisfy your 'cue craving. If you filled up on sides and couldn't finish the ribs, see the ideas below for how to make them anew on day two.

Serves 1 generously or 2 with sides

- 1 (1- to 1½-pound) half rack baby back ribs (see Note)
- 1 teaspoon kosher salt
- 1 teaspoon onion powder
- ½ teaspoon freshly ground black pepper
- ½ teaspoon smoked paprika
- ⅓ cup barbecue sauce, store-bought or homemade (page 139)

1. Preheat the oven to 275°F.
2. Keep the ribs whole—we're not slicing them yet! Pat the ribs dry, then place them on a rimmed baking sheet and sprinkle all over with the salt, onion powder, pepper, and paprika. Cover tightly with aluminum foil and bake for 2½ to 3 hours, until the meat is tender and you can easily wiggle the end of a bone.
3. Remove the ribs from the oven and discard the foil. Carefully pour off any fat on the baking sheet. Move the rack to the top position and turn the oven to broil (on high, if that's an option).
4. Brush the barbecue sauce all over the ribs and broil with the meaty side up for 3 to 5 minutes (but every broiler is different, so keep an eye on it), until the glaze is sticky and charred in spots. Slice and eat up.

What to do with leftover ribs: First of all, wow. You didn't finish this? Okay. Maybe you had a big lunch. Anyway, pull the meat from the bones, and you basically have pulled pork. Make a pulled pork sandwich, tacos, or a quesadilla. Simmer with more barbecue sauce and use as a saucy topping for grits or a baked potato. Or crisp it up with potatoes for a breakfast hash.

Note

Some stores will sell you a half rack; that's what you want! If all you can find is a full rack, then cut it in half and freeze one half for another time. Or double the recipe and use it all now.

Beef and Broccoli and You

A famously easy dish, now portioned to have for dinner with a friend or lunch the next day. No fancy bells and whistles here, just meat and potatoes. Except the meat is flank steak and the potatoes are broccoli. If you're feeling adventurous, you can also make rice from scratch to serve alongside, but if you're lazy like me, pair this with one of those Minute Rice Cups that come in packs of four.

Serves 2

1 (8-ounce) flank steak

⅛ teaspoon baking soda

1 teaspoon plus 1 tablespoon oyster sauce

1½ teaspoons cornstarch

1 small head broccoli, crown cut into 1-inch florets and stem cut into ½-inch-thick slices

1 tablespoon soy sauce

½ teaspoon chicken bouillon paste (or use 2 tablespoons chicken broth and skip the water)

1 tablespoon vegetable oil, such as canola

2 garlic cloves, minced

1 (1-inch) piece fresh ginger, peeled and minced

½ teaspoon toasted sesame oil

1 teaspoon sesame seeds, toasted, for garnish

Rice for One (page 130), or 1 cup cooked white or brown rice, for serving

1. Slice the steak in half lengthwise with the grain, then into ¼-inch-thick slices on a diagonal against the grain. Place it in a medium bowl and add 1 tablespoon water and the baking soda. Massage the mixture into the beef (this helps tenderize the meat). Add 1 teaspoon of the oyster sauce and ½ teaspoon of the cornstarch and toss again. Let stand for 30 minutes.

2. Meanwhile, place the broccoli and ¼ cup water in a large skillet. Bring the water to a simmer over medium heat, then cover the pan and cook, shaking the pan regularly, until the broccoli is bright green and crisp-tender, 5 to 7 minutes. Drain the broccoli in a colander.

3. In a small bowl, whisk together 2 tablespoons water, the remaining 1 tablespoon oyster sauce, the soy sauce, and bouillon paste until smooth. In a separate small bowl, whisk together the remaining 1 teaspoon cornstarch and 2 tablespoons water until smooth.

4. In the skillet you used for the broccoli, heat the vegetable oil over medium-high heat for 1 minute. Add a piece of beef to the pan—if it sizzles immediately, the oil is hot enough; if not, wait a minute and try again. Spread the beef into a single layer and cook, undisturbed, until golden on the bottom, 3 minutes, then stir and cook, stirring often, just until you see no pink, 1 to 2 minutes more. Transfer the beef to a plate, leaving the fat in the pan.

5. Add the garlic and ginger to the pan and cook, stirring continuously, until fragrant, about 30 seconds. Remove the pan from the heat, pour in the sauce, and scrape up the browned bits from the bottom of the pan. Return the pan to medium heat and bring the sauce to a simmer, then pour the cornstarch mixture into the sauce and stir to combine. Add the beef and juices and the broccoli to the pan and cook, stirring continuously, until the sauce thickens and coats everything evenly, 1 to 2 minutes. If the sauce is too thin, simmer it for a bit longer; if it's too thick, add water 1 teaspoon at a time. Stir in the sesame oil.

6. Sprinkle with the sesame seeds and serve with rice.

Under the Tuscan Chicken

In the 2003 romantic comedy film/1996 memoir *Under the Tuscan Sun*, a San Francisco writer's life takes a turn when she discovers her husband's been cheating on her. Booooo! At the urging of her friend, she takes a trip to Tuscany, and, on her own for the first time in a long time, her life is forever changed. Yay!!!! While we can't all book a last-minute trip to Italy, you can forever change your life by having Tuscany in your own kitchen. Hold on to your butts, fellow lactose intolerators—this is a juicy chicken dish draped in a very creamy sauce that'll have you shouting "Help, help, my pants are filling with gas!" in fluent Italian.

Serves 1

1 small boneless, skinless chicken breast (about 8 ounces)

½ teaspoon dried oregano or Italian seasoning

½ teaspoon kosher salt

¼ teaspoon garlic powder

⅛ teaspoon red pepper flakes

⅛ teaspoon freshly ground black pepper

1 tablespoon extra-virgin olive oil

1 tablespoon unsalted butter

1 large or 2 small garlic cloves, grated

Handful of cherry tomatoes, halved

2 handfuls of baby spinach

¼ cup freshly grated Parmigiano Reggiano cheese, plus more for serving

¼ cup heavy cream

1. Place the chicken breast on a cutting board and hold it in place with the palm of your nondominant hand. Use a sharp knife to carefully cut parallel to the cutting board so you cut the chicken into two thin cutlets. Place the cutlets in a small bowl and add the oregano, salt, garlic powder, red pepper flakes, and black pepper and toss to coat.

2. Heat the olive oil in a medium skillet over medium heat until it shimmers, about 2 minutes. Add the chicken and cook, undisturbed, until it comes off the pan easily and is golden on the bottom, 3 to 4 minutes, then flip the cutlets. Cook until golden on the second side and cooked through (if you cut into one, there should be no pink inside), 2 to 3 minutes. Transfer the chicken to a plate to rest.

3. Add the butter and grated garlic to the skillet and stir immediately to melt the butter. When you can smell the garlic, about 30 seconds, add the tomatoes and 2 tablespoons water and cook, scraping up the browned bits from the bottom of the pan with your spoon, just until the tomatoes start to collapse, about 1 minute. Add the spinach and reduce the heat to medium-low. Cook, stirring often, until the spinach wilts, about 2 minutes.

4. Stir in the cheese and cream. Return the chicken and any accumulated juices to the skillet and nestle it into the sauce. Simmer until the sauce thickens slightly and coats the back of a spoon, 1 to 2 minutes. Serve the chicken with the sauce poured on top and more cheese grated over.

Green Enchiladas

I'll be honest because we're friends: I do not like enchiladas. I don't like when things are in a lot of sauce, and apparently that's what makes an enchilada good. Because I am selfless, I didn't want my dislike to prevent you from satisfying your smaller-serving-enchilada craving, so here it is! I begged my friend and Enchilada Master, Maddie, to try this (jk, she offered), and she said, "Wow, yum," so trust a stranger's best friend that these are good. This makes about a cup of sauce, but if you don't want to make it from scratch, go with the good lord and use store-bought.

Serves 1

3 medium tomatillos, husked, rinsed, and quartered

¼ small white onion (see Note)

1 serrano chile, or ½ jalapeño

1 garlic clove, peeled

4 sprigs cilantro

½ teaspoon kosher salt

Juice of ½ lime

2 tablespoons vegetable oil, such as canola

2 (6-inch) corn tortillas

1 cup shredded rotisserie chicken, shredded Oaxaca or mozzarella cheese, leftover carnitas (see page 124), or a mix!

Pinch of freshly ground black pepper (optional)

¼ cup crumbled Cotija cheese

Sour cream, for serving

1. Preheat the oven to 350°F.

2. Place the tomatillos, onion, chile, and garlic in a small skillet over high heat. Cook the vegetables, turning them occasionally, until they are a little blackened on all sides, 6 to 8 minutes. Transfer the charred tomatillos, onion, and garlic to a blender (or a tall container, if using an immersion blender). Remove the serrano stem (and the seeds, if you don't like too much spice). Add the chile to the blender along with 3 sprigs of cilantro, the salt, and the lime juice. Blend on medium-high speed until smooth, about 1 minute. Pour half the salsa into a loaf pan or a small baking dish that's at least 6 × 4 inches.

3. In the same skillet, heat the oil over medium heat for a couple of minutes. Add a tortilla to the pan—if it sizzles gently, the oil is hot enough; if not, you can leave the tortilla in there and just add a little cooking time. Fry the tortilla until it's softened, about 10 seconds per side. Use tongs to remove it, let the excess oil drip back into the pan, and transfer it to a plate. Repeat with the remaining tortilla.

4. Place one tortilla on your work surface, add half the filling of your choice (I like to add a pinch of black pepper to chicken or carnitas), and roll it shut. Place the enchilada in the baking pan, seam-side down, and repeat with the other tortilla and the rest of the filling. Pour the remaining salsa on top and sprinkle with the Cotija cheese.

5. Bake for 20 to 25 minutes, until the sauce is bubbling around the edges. Remove from the oven and let cool for 5 minutes. Meanwhile, pick the leaves from the remaining cilantro sprig.

6. Sprinkle the cilantro on top of the enchiladas, add a dollop of sour cream, and serve.

Note

If you like raw onion on your enchiladas, cut a few thin slices for garnish from the other half.

Spicy

& Hot

Spicy Pork Lettuce D-Cups

All dressed up and nowhere to go—that's how these lettuce cups feel, and they're delighted by it. You and the crisped pork can enjoy a classy night in as you both revel in the evening topless, showing off those D-cups to no one.

Serves 1

- 2 garlic cloves, grated
- 1 (1-inch) piece fresh ginger, peeled and grated
- 1 small fresh red chile, such as bird's eye or serrano, grated
- 2 tablespoons soy sauce
- Juice of ½ lime, plus more if needed
- 1 teaspoon vegetable oil, such as canola
- 8 ounces ground pork (not lean)
- ¼ teaspoon light brown sugar
- ⅛ teaspoon kosher salt
- Pinch of freshly ground black pepper
- 8 to 10 butter lettuce leaves
- 1 Persian (mini) cucumber, halved crosswise and cut into thin matchsticks
- 2 scallions, thinly sliced on an angle
- Small handful of fresh cilantro (about ½ cup loosely packed), coarsely chopped
- Leaves from 1 sprig mint, Thai basil, or Italian basil, larger leaves torn

1. In a small bowl, combine the garlic, ginger, and chile. Add the soy sauce and the lime juice. Taste the sauce and see if you want more lime juice—it should be punchy.

2. Heat the oil in a medium skillet over medium-high heat for 1 minute. Add a piece of pork to the pan—if it sizzles immediately, the oil is hot enough; if not, wait a minute and try again. Add all the pork, break it up into smaller chunks, then spread it out into an even layer and cook, undisturbed, until browned and crisp on the bottom, 3 to 4 minutes. Stir the pork and cook, undisturbed, until browned on the second side, 3 to 4 minutes more. Stir again, then cook, breaking up the pork into small pieces, until the pork is crumbled and you see no pink left, about 1 minute more.

3. Season the pork with the brown sugar, salt, and pepper. Pour in the sauce and cook, stirring often, until the sauce is reduced and no longer runny, about 1 minute. Remove from the heat.

4. To serve, stack 2 lettuce leaves, add a heaping spoonful of pork, then top with cucumber, scallion, and herbs. Repeat with the remaining ingredients to make 4 or 5 cups. Dig in.

Pineapple-Chipotle Salmon

A little sweet, a little spicy, that's how this salmon differs from his BBQ and teriyaki buddies. He wanted to grow up to be more than just a fish in sauce—he wanted to be rubbed in a spicy chipotle chile powder and topped with a ring of fresh pineapple. He's a reminder that we should always dream big.

Serves 1

½ to 1 teaspoon chipotle chile powder, depending on how much spice you like

¼ teaspoon kosher salt, plus more as needed

¼ teaspoon garlic powder

¼ teaspoon dried oregano

⅛ teaspoon ground cumin

1 (6-ounce) salmon fillet, preferably about 1 inch thick, thawed if frozen

2 teaspoons vegetable oil, such as canola

1 canned pineapple ring, or 1 (¼-inch-thick) fresh pineapple ring

¼ teaspoon light brown sugar

Side of choice

1. Preheat the oven to 450°F. Position a rack 6 inches away from the broiler heating element. Line a small baking sheet with aluminum foil.

2. In a small bowl, mix the chile powder, salt, garlic powder, oregano, and cumin. Pat the salmon dry with paper towels. Place it on the prepared baking sheet and coat all over with the oil, then season it generously, all over, with the spice mix, brushing any excess off.

3. Place the salmon skin-side down (if it has skin) on the baking sheet and put the pineapple ring on top of it, then sprinkle the pineapple with the brown sugar and a pinch of salt.

4. Bake for 10 to 12 minutes for medium or about 15 minutes for well-done, then check to see if the salmon flakes easily with a fork. Switch the oven to broil and broil for about 2 minutes to crisp the pineapple just a bit. Serve right away with a side. (I'm keen on green beans, but by all means, do what your plate deems.)

Migas

Migas is a traditional Spanish and Portuguese dish, and the word *migas* means "crumbs" in Spanish, which is endearing. This recipe leans more into the Mexican version by using crispy, crumbled tortilla chips. This will serve one, so tell your *a*-migas they will have to make their own crumbs.

Serves 1

1 small plum tomato, chopped (about 3/4 cup)

Kosher salt

2 large eggs

1 tablespoon unsalted butter

1/2 small yellow onion, or 1 medium shallot, finely chopped (about 1/2 cup)

1/2 jalapeño, or 1 serrano chile, finely chopped (leave some or all the seeds in depending on how much spice you like)

1 cup lightly crushed tostadas or salted tortilla chips

2 (6-inch) or 3 (4-inch) corn tortillas, warmed

1/4 ripe but firm avocado, sliced

Leaves from 2 sprigs cilantro, coarsely chopped (about 1 tablespoon)

Crumbled Cotija cheese, for serving (optional)

Salsa or hot sauce, for serving

1. Place the tomato in a colander over the sink and add a pinch of salt. Let drain for a few minutes so the juices don't make your eggs soggy.

2. In a small bowl, whisk together the eggs, 1 tablespoon water (if you like a soft scramble, which I do), and a pinch of salt until completely smooth and no streaks of egg white remain.

3. Melt the butter in a small or medium nonstick skillet (the "nonstick" is the most important part) over medium heat. When the butter is foaming, add the onion and jalapeño. Cook, stirring often, until the onion is soft and translucent but before it has taken on any color, 2 to 4 minutes.

4. Pour in the egg and immediately reduce the heat to low. Scramble the eggs for just 5 seconds, stirring in a figure-eight motion with your spatula just twice, then add two-thirds of the tortilla chips and the tomatoes and cook, stirring continuously, until the eggs are just set and the chips have softened, 1 to 2 minutes more. Fold in the remaining chips.

5. Divide the migas between the tortillas, then top with the avocado, cilantro, Cotija (if using), and some sort of spicy sauce to get your fix.

How Now Brown Kung Pao Chicken

I had a lisp growing up, so I wouldn't have been able to say "Sichuan," which is the Chinese province where kung pao chicken originated. As part of my speech therapy, I was forced to say "How Now Brown Cow," and this proves that time is a flat circle. Sichuan peppercorns are tingly, slightly numbing, and not always included in kung pao, so they're optional. I am a wimp about spice, so I will never have peppercorns, but you absolutely should if that's your jam. While the dish traditionally uses whole dried chiles (something that would probably bring back the lisp), this one uses the more available red pepper flakes; add more of them if you like lots of . . . pao! This isn't overly spicy, but should more spice be desired, simply sprinkle more red pepper flakes into the simmering pot. Try saying that three times fast!

Serves 1

1 small boneless, skinless chicken breast (8 ounces), cut into ½-inch cubes

3 teaspoons soy sauce

¾ teaspoon cornstarch

½ teaspoon red pepper flakes

¼ teaspoon kosher salt, plus more as needed

1½ tablespoons black vinegar or balsamic vinegar

2 teaspoons sugar

1 tablespoon vegetable oil, such as canola

1 bell pepper (any color), cut into ½-inch cubes

1 big garlic clove, finely chopped

¼ teaspoon crushed Sichuan peppercorns, or ⅛ teaspoon ground Sichuan peppercorns (optional)

3 tablespoons roasted salted peanuts

Rice for One (page 130), or 1 cup cooked white or brown rice, for serving

1. In a medium bowl, stir together the chicken, 1½ teaspoons of the soy sauce, ½ teaspoon of the cornstarch, ¼ teaspoon of the red pepper flakes, and the salt. In a second medium bowl, stir together the vinegar, sugar, remaining 1½ teaspoons soy sauce, remaining ¼ teaspoon cornstarch, and remaining ¼ teaspoon red pepper flakes until smooth.

2. Heat the oil in a nonstick medium skillet over medium-high heat for 1 minute. Add a piece of bell pepper to the pan—if it sizzles immediately, the oil is hot enough; if not, wait a minute and try again. Add the rest of the bell pepper and cook, stirring just once or twice, until bright in color and browned in spots, 2 to 3 minutes. Using tongs or a slotted spoon, transfer the peppers to the bowl of sauce, leaving the oil in the pan, and season with a pinch of salt.

3. Add the chicken to the skillet in a single layer. Reduce the heat to medium and cook, undisturbed, until browned on the bottom, 2 to 3 minutes. Add the garlic and Sichuan peppercorns (if using). Cook, stirring continuously, until the chicken is opaque all over and the garlic is fragrant, 1 to 2 minutes.

4. Give the peppers and sauce a stir, then add them and the peanuts to the skillet and stir until glazed and glossy, 1 to 2 minutes. Eat with rice!

Shopping tip: Meet your butcher, who will sling you a breast or two instead of a huge pack.

Butter Tofu Just fo' You

This is a vegetarian twist on the Indian dish murgh makhani. Here, tofu has the ride of its life in a simmery yogurt-infused marinade.

Serves 1

Tofu

½ cup plain full-fat Greek yogurt

1 garlic clove, grated

1 (½-inch) piece fresh ginger, peeled and grated

½ to 1 teaspoon Kashmiri chile powder (depending on how much spice you like; or use hot paprika and a pinch of cayenne pepper)

½ teaspoon garam masala

½ teaspoon kosher salt

⅛ teaspoon ground turmeric

8 ounces medium-firm tofu, pressed (see Note) and cut into bite-size cubes (about ¾ inch)

Sauce

1 tablespoon unsalted butter

½ small yellow onion, or 1 medium shallot, finely chopped (about ½ cup)

1 heaping teaspoon tomato paste

½ teaspoon chicken bouillon paste or vegetarian bouillon paste

¼ cup heavy cream

For Serving

Rice for One (page 130), or 1 cup cooked white or brown rice

Leaves from 1 sprig cilantro, coarsely chopped

1. **Marinate the tofu:** In a small bowl, whisk together the yogurt, garlic, ginger, chile powder, garam masala, salt, and turmeric until smooth. Add the tofu and gently fold it into the marinade with a spatula; you want the cubes to be coated but not broken up. Cover the bowl and refrigerate for at least 1 hour or ideally overnight.

2. **When you're ready to eat, make the sauce:** Melt the butter in a medium skillet (nonstick, if you've got it) over medium heat. When the butter is foaming, add the onion. Cook, stirring often, until the onion is browned on the edges, 5 to 7 minutes. Add the tofu and all the marinade (scrape the bowl—that's where the flavor is!). Cook, stirring as little as possible to encourage browning, until the marinade has reduced and you can see the oil separating from the yogurt mixture, about 5 minutes.

3. Pour in ½ cup water and add the tomato paste and bouillon paste. Stir to combine and dissolve the pastes. Reduce the heat to medium-low and simmer, swirling the pan occasionally, until the sauce has reduced and the oils start to rise to the top again, 7 to 10 minutes. Stir in the cream and simmer until the sauce coats the back of a spoon, 2 to 3 minutes.

4. Spoon the tofu and sauce over rice, sprinkle with the cilantro, and dig in.

Note

To press tofu, wrap it in paper towels and put it into a colander with a flat bottom or on a plate. Put another plate on top of it, then put something heavy on the plate, like a big can of tomatoes. Let it press for 30 to 60 minutes, then discard the paper towel. Your tofu is now ready to soak up marinade!

Double the Dan Noodles

I have many friends named Dan, but two LA ones in particular are not only nice guys but super hot. Like, washboard abs, windswept hair, and winning smiles. Their birthdays are around the same time, so they like to throw a "Double Dan" birthday party for and with each other each year. While this recipe is enough for a singular Dan, it still has double the fun and double the hotness, just like a Double Dan party. Careful, though: The chile oil brings the heat. You may need to go to a Chinese supermarket to find some of the ingredients, but the Chinese sesame paste is so delicious, it's worth the effort.

Serves 1

Sauce

2 tablespoons Chinese sesame paste or tahini

1 tablespoon chile crisp or chile oil

1 tablespoon soy sauce

1 tablespoon rice vinegar

½ teaspoon sugar

1 garlic clove, grated

Pinch of ground Sichuan peppercorns (optional)

Noodles

2 teaspoons kosher salt

3 ounces dried wheat noodles (usually 1 bundle of noodles, or even spaghetti will work)

2 teaspoons vegetable oil, such as canola

4 ounces ground pork (not lean) or ground beef

¼ cup chopped preserved mustard greens or sour pickled mustard greens

1 tablespoon soy sauce

1 scallion, white and green parts separated and thinly sliced

Pinch of ground Sichuan peppercorns (optional)

1. **Make the sauce:** In a small bowl, whisk together the sesame paste, chile crisp, soy sauce, vinegar, sugar, garlic, and Sichuan pepper (if using). It may not be totally smooth yet, but that's fine.

2. **Make the noodles:** Bring 4 cups water to a boil in a small pot over high heat. Add the salt, then add the noodles and cook according to the package directions. Scoop out ¼ cup of the cooking water and set it aside, then drain the noodles.

3. Whisk 1 tablespoon of the reserved cooking water into the sauce; if it's not smooth, add more cooking water a splash at a time until it is.

4. Heat the vegetable oil in a medium skillet over medium-high heat for a couple of minutes. Add a piece of pork to the pan—if it sizzles immediately, the oil is hot enough; if not, wait a minute and try again. Add all the pork and break it up into smaller chunks, then spread it out into an even layer and cook, undisturbed, until browned and crisp on the bottom, 3 to 4 minutes. Stir the pork, then cook, undisturbed, until browned on the second side, 3 to 4 minutes more. Stir again, then cook, breaking up the meat into small pieces, until the pork is crumbled and you see no pink left, 1 to 2 minutes more.

5. Add the mustard greens, soy sauce, scallion whites, and Sichuan pepper (if using) and stir to combine. Cook until the pork is completely cooked through and the meat is dry and crumbly, 1 minute.

6. To serve, put the noodles in a bowl, top with the meat mixture, then pour over the sauce. Stir everything together, then garnish with the scallion greens and enjoy.

Note

If you don't want to buy a half gallon of buttermilk just to use ¼ cup (though it does last a very long time), mix ¼ cup whole milk with ¾ teaspoon fresh lemon juice or distilled white vinegar. Let it sit for 10 minutes, after which it should be curdled, tangy, and ready to use.

Nashville Hot Chicken Tendies Sandwich

If you're in the mood for hot poultry but want to skip the chaos of Nashville—known for its music scene and recently crowned the Bachelorette Capital of America—I've got you covered. Covered like these chicken tendies are with a cacophony of things to make your mouth sizzle like the singer-songwriters at Tequila Cowboy on Broadway.

Serves 1

- ¼ cup buttermilk (see Note)
- 1 tablespoon brine from your favorite jar of dill pickles
- 1 teaspoon hot sauce
- 1⅛ teaspoons kosher salt
- ⅛ teaspoon freshly ground black pepper
- 3 chicken breast tenders
- ½ cup all-purpose flour
- Vegetable oil, such as canola, for frying
- 1 teaspoon light brown sugar
- ½ teaspoon cayenne pepper, plus more as needed
- ½ teaspoon chili powder
- ½ teaspoon garlic powder
- ¼ teaspoon smoked paprika
- 2 slices white sandwich bread
- Dill pickle slices, for serving
- Coleslaw, store-bought or homemade (page 143), for serving (optional, but recommended)

1. In a medium bowl, whisk together the buttermilk, pickle brine, hot sauce, ½ teaspoon of the salt, and the black pepper until well combined. Add the chicken tenders and toss to coat. Cover the bowl and refrigerate for at least 4 hours or up to overnight.

2. When you're ready to fry the tendies, place the flour and ½ teaspoon of the salt in a shallow dish and stir to combine. Working with one tender at a time, remove the chicken from the marinade (don't throw out the marinade!) and let any excess drip off. Dip it in flour to coat, then shake off the excess. Dip it back in the marinade to cover, let the excess drip off again, then toss in the flour one more time. Transfer the breaded chicken to a plate and repeat with the other tenders.

3. Fill a medium skillet (cast iron, if you've got it) with ¼ inch of oil. Heat the oil over medium-high heat until a pinch of flour sizzles immediately on contact (about 325°F, if you have a thermometer). Set a wire rack over a baking sheet or line a plate with paper towels.

4. Add the breaded chicken to the hot oil and fry, turning occasionally, until golden brown and crispy all over and cooked through (a thermometer should read 165°F), 6 to 8 minutes total. Transfer the tenders to the rack as they finish cooking and let them rest while you make the sauce.

5. In a small heatproof bowl, combine the brown sugar, cayenne, chili powder, garlic powder, paprika, and remaining ⅛ teaspoon salt. Carefully use a heatproof spoon to add 2 tablespoons of the frying oil to the bowl. Stir to combine. At this point, the mixture should be just warm, but check the temperature before you taste it! Use the spoon to taste a little and add more cayenne until it's as spicy as you like. Brush the sauce all over the tenders.

6. Place the chicken tenders on a slice of bread, top with pickles, then the other slice of bread, and serve immediately, ideally with some coleslaw on the side.

Pork and Chile Crisp Dumplings

Dumplings are a craving that comes up often for me, so here's a pro tip: Buy a whole package of dumpling wrappers and increase the filling amount to finish the package, then freeze the rest. You'll have dumplings for a month. Or a week. Or a day. Depending on how strong your dumpling willpower is.

Makes 12 to 14 dumplings

1 sweet or hot Italian sausage, casing removed, or 3 ounces ground pork

1 tablespoon Shaoxing wine, sherry, or water

1 tablespoon plus 1 teaspoon chile crisp

1 tablespoon plus 1 teaspoon soy sauce

1 scallion, white and green parts separated and very thinly sliced

12 to 14 (4-inch) round dumpling wrappers

2 tablespoons vegetable oil, such as canola

2 teaspoons black vinegar or balsamic vinegar

1. In a small bowl, combine the sausage, Shaoxing wine, 1 tablespoon of the chile crisp, 1 tablespoon of the soy sauce, and the scallion whites. Use your hand (you can wear a glove) to mix until everything is evenly combined.

2. Fill a small bowl with water. Line a plate with parchment paper.

3. Lay one dumpling wrapper in the palm of your nondominant hand. Place a heaping teaspoon of the filling in the center. Wet your other index finger in the water and brush the edge of the dumpling wrapper so it's damp. Fold the top of the wrapper over and press it to seal just in the center. Press out any air around the filling, then use your thumb and forefinger to crimp the dough: Starting on one side of the center, push about ¼ inch of just the top half of the wrapper toward the center, then press it into the bottom wrapper to create a pleat (so you're pleating just one half of the seal, keeping the other smooth, which is what creates the crescent shape). Repeat all the way to one end, then repeat on the other side of the center, crimping toward the center again. Place the dumpling on the plate with the pleat running across the top and press gently to create a flat bottom. Repeat with the remaining filling and wrappers. (You can freeze some of the dumplings at this point, if you like. Stick the plate in the freezer, making sure the dumplings aren't touching, and freeze until solid, about 4 hours. Transfer the dumplings to a zip-top bag and store in the freezer for up to 3 months. Cook from frozen as directed below, adding a minute or two to the steaming time to make sure they cook through.)

4. Line a plate with paper towels. Heat the oil in a medium skillet over medium-high heat for 1 minute. Add a dumpling to the pan, flat-side down—if it sizzles immediately, the oil is hot enough; if not, wait a minute and try again. Add all the dumplings and cook until they're crisp on the bottom, 2 to 3 minutes, then cover the pan with a tight-fitting lid. Crack the lid away from you, pour in 2 tablespoons water, and immediately cover again. Cook, undisturbed, until all the water has cooked off and you hear sizzling again, 2 to 3 minutes. Uncover and cook until any remaining water has evaporated and the dumplings lift easily from the pan, 30 to 60 seconds more. Transfer the dumplings to the paper towel–lined plate to drain.

5. In a small serving bowl, mix the remaining 1 teaspoon chile crisp, remaining 1 teaspoon soy sauce, and the vinegar. Transfer the dumplings to a serving plate and sprinkle with the scallion greens. Enjoy with the dipping sauce!

Nice &

Sweet

Strawberry Shawtycake

According to all rap music, to be a shawty means you're either a young attractive woman or someone who is shorter than most people. Like the latter, this is a single-layer biscuit from scratch (!!) that sandwiches fresh homemade whipped cream and sweetened sliced strawberries for the shawty-est of cakes.

Makes 1 shortcake

Biscuit

½ cup all-purpose flour, plus more for dusting

1 teaspoon granulated sugar, plus more as needed

½ teaspoon baking powder

⅛ teaspoon kosher salt

2 tablespoons unsalted butter, cut into small cubes

3 tablespoons heavy cream, plus more for brushing

Strawberries

Handful of ripe, beautiful strawberries (about 6 small), hulled and thinly sliced lengthwise

½ teaspoon granulated sugar, plus more if needed

Whipped Cream

3 tablespoons heavy cream

1 heaping teaspoon powdered sugar

¼ teaspoon pure vanilla extract

1. Preheat the oven to 450°F.

2. **Make the biscuit:** In a small bowl, combine the flour, 1 teaspoon of the granulated sugar, the baking powder, and salt and mix with a fork until well combined. Add the butter cubes and, using a fork or a pastry cutter, break them down and work them into the flour until the whole mixture looks crumbly, almost like damp sand, and there are no pockets of completely dry flour and no more than a few pea-size pieces of butter. If at any point the butter starts to soften and warm, stick the whole bowl in the freezer for 10 minutes, then keep going.

3. Pour the cream into the mixture. Knead it in the bowl until a soft dough forms and there are no loose bits of flour, about 1 minute. Turn the dough out onto a small piece of parchment paper. Gently press it into a ½-inch-thick rectangle. Trim each side with a sharp knife so they're straight and flat and discard the scraps. Cut the dough in half crosswise to make two squarish pieces. Place the biscuits (still on the parchment) on a plate and freeze it for 15 minutes.

4. **Meanwhile, make the strawberries:** Place the strawberries in a small bowl, sprinkle with the granulated sugar, and toss. Taste one; if your strawberries aren't particularly sweet, add more sugar a pinch at a time until they taste delightful to you. Set aside to let the sugar work its magic on the strawberries.

5. **Back to the biscuits:** Brush a splash (around ¼ teaspoon) of cream on the top of each biscuit. Stack the two biscuits, then sprinkle the top with ¼ teaspoon granulated sugar.

6. Bake for about 20 minutes, until the biscuit is golden brown and set on the top. Transfer it to a wire rack to cool until warm, about 10 minutes.

7. **Make the whipped cream:** Place the cream, powdered sugar, and vanilla in a small jar. Screw on the lid tightly and shake like crazy until you don't hear any more liquid sloshing around. Stop as soon as you get to this point and check—you're looking for softly whipped cream, not butter, so move cautiously after this point. Keep shaking until the cream doesn't move in the jar.

8. To serve, carefully split the biscuit in half horizontally. Spoon the strawberries and as much of the juices in the bowl as you'd like onto the bottom half, then spoon over the whipped cream. Add the biscuit top and eat immediately.

Nice Krispie Treats

Picture it: the year was 1993, and the world was on the cusp of global transformation: The European Union was founded, *Jurassic Park* premiered, and Kellogg's introduced the world's best cereal, Rice Krispie Treats Cereal. It was a cavity waiting to happen. Rice Krispies Treats Cereal, with its crispy, sugary clusters, was officially discontinued in 2019, and I miss them every day, but your favorite cereal never really dies as long as it lives on in your memories. It's not the same, of course, but you can make your *own* Rice Krispies Treat, though every other recipe is meant to make enough to feed a youth soccer team. If I eat more than two, I want to barf, but no barfing here, as this is just enough to satisfy the craving. This is great for celebrating getting out of a sticky situation and putting one into your mouth instead. For my gluten-free friends, you'll want to use a brand other than Kellogg's Rice Krispies—any gluten-free crispy rice cereal will do.

Makes 2 regular treats or 4 small treats

2 tablespoons unsalted butter, plus more for greasing

1¼ cups mini marshmallows

1½ cups Rice Krispies or other crispy toasted rice cereal

¼ teaspoon kosher salt

Rainbow sprinkles (optional, but recommended)

1. Butter a 7½ × 6-inch baking dish, or two 1-cup ramekins.
2. Melt the butter in a medium saucepan over medium heat, then cook, stirring frequently, until nutty-smelling and golden brown, 2 to 3 minutes. Immediately reduce the heat to low so the butter doesn't burn and stir in the marshmallows. When the marshmallows have melted, add the cereal and salt and stir quickly to combine. Eat a spoonful of the warm, gooey crispies—delicious.
3. Transfer the mixture to the buttered half of the pan and very gently spread it with a spatula into an even layer so it forms a square, pressing down very lightly to help shape it and evening out the end. Top with sprinkles, if desired. Let cool completely, about 30 minutes, then cut in half and enjoy, or rip into with your bare hands.

Flavor Variations

S'mores: Use graham cracker cereal (like Golden Grahams) and add chocolate chips at the end.

Nutella: Stir in a spoonful of Nutella after the marshmallows have melted. Add some chopped toasted hazelnuts, too, if you're feeling it.

Peanut butter coconut: Use peanut butter Panda Puffs or another peanutty cereal and add chocolate chips and toasted coconut chips at the end.

Cereal swap: What do you have? You could probably make treats with them. Favorites include Corn Pops, Frosted Flakes, and Cinnamon Toast Crunch.

Banana Puddin'

How do you solve wanting dessert but it's a hot summer day? Or you naturally run warm? Or you're having a menopausal hot flash? Or your poorly ventilated kitchen is hot from testing recipes for your cookbook? The answer is no-cook banana pudding! Patience is the name of the game with puddings from scratch, but it'll be beautifully layered with banana and mini Nillas.

Serves 2

½ cup whole milk

2 tablespoons instant vanilla pudding mix (from a 3.4-ounce box)

About 25 mini Nilla wafers

1 ripe banana, thinly sliced

3 tablespoons heavy cream

1 heaping teaspoon powdered sugar

¼ teaspoon pure vanilla extract

1. In a small bowl, combine the milk and instant pudding mix and whisk with a fork until completely smooth. Refrigerate for 15 minutes to set.

2. Grab a ramekin or a small serving bowl (whatever you use should hold 1½ to 2 cups). Cover the bottom with a layer of Nilla wafers, then top with a layer of banana slices. If you really love bananas, it's okay if they overlap a bit. Spread half the pudding on top. Repeat to make another layer of wafers, then banana, then the rest of the pudding, then top with another layer of wafers and a final layer of banana. Save any extra wafers for decoration (the bananas will brown, so you can just eat those or freeze them). Cover the dish with plastic wrap pressed against the surface. Refrigerate until the flavors have melded and the cookies have softened, at least 2 hours or up to 6 hours.

3. When you're ready to serve, place the cream, powdered sugar, and vanilla in a small jar. Screw on the lid tightly and shake like crazy until you don't hear any more liquid sloshing around. Stop as soon as you get to this point and check—you're looking for softly whipped cream, not butter, so move cautiously after this point. Keep shaking until the cream doesn't move when you open the jar.

4. Top the pudding with the whipped cream, garnish with the remaining wafers, and enjoy!

Peanut (the Dog) Butter Cookie

Did you know it takes about 540 peanuts to make one 12-ounce jar of peanut butter? Well, now you do. Did you know the dog I adopted in April 2020 is named Peanut? Well, now you do. Much like my 9-pound Chihuahua mix, these peanut butter cookies have crisp outsides that give way to a sandy-fudgy middle. They're nutty, salty, and sweet (also like my dog) and only require four ingredients: brown sugar, peanut butter, egg, and flaky sea salt for topping. Four ingredients seems suspicious, I know, but you're not my dog and I'm not a delivery driver knocking at your door—you can trust me.

Makes 4 cookies

7 tablespoons packed light brown sugar

1 large egg yolk

7 tablespoons creamy peanut butter (not natural peanut butter, the kind with additives)

Flaky salt, for sprinkling

1. Preheat the oven to 350°F. Line a quarter sheet pan with parchment paper.

2. In a medium bowl, combine the brown sugar, egg yolk, and 2 teaspoons water and stir vigorously with a spatula until smooth. Add the peanut butter and stir until combined and smooth.

3. Use the spatula to portion the dough into 4 cookies, using about 2 heaping tablespoons of dough for each. Transfer them to the prepared baking sheet, leaving a few inches between each, and smooth any wonky edges to make the cookies round. Sprinkle lightly with flaky salt.

4. Bake for 18 to 20 minutes, until matte all over and golden on the edges. Remove from the oven and let cool slightly in the pan. Eat them warm or fully cooled.

Pardon My French Toast

Les français are back for breakfast! A sweet way to get the day going, two brioche slices of toast sitting in your tummy will give you the confidence to start your day curious and be ready to, _pardon my French_, fuck around and find out. Use stale bread, because fresh bread will absorb too much liquid and collapse after cooking. If you don't have stale bread and you're a planner, you can leave your slices out overnight. If you're not, you can bake them in a 300°F oven for about 15 minutes, flipping once, to dry them out, then let them cool before proceeding. _Bonne chance!_

Serves 1

⅓ cup half-and-half

1 large egg

1 tablespoon granulated sugar

½ teaspoon pure vanilla extract

⅛ teaspoon kosher salt

2 thick slices stale brioche bread

1 tablespoon unsalted butter

A pat of butter, maple syrup, and/or powdered sugar, for serving

1. Set a wire rack over a baking sheet. In a shallow dish large enough to fit a slice of the bread, combine the half-and-half, egg, granulated sugar, vanilla, and salt. Whisk until completely smooth, with no streaks of egg white remaining (this is important so you don't get bits of cooked egg on your toast).

2. Dip one slice of bread into the custard and let it soak until saturated, about 10 seconds per side. Use a fork or spatula to lift the bread out of the egg mixture, letting any excess drip back into the dish, and put it on the rack. Repeat with the other slice.

3. Melt the butter in a medium skillet over medium heat. When the butter is foaming, swirl it around the pan so it evenly coats the bottom. Add the bread to the pan and fry until beautifully browned on the bottom, adjusting the heat if it's browning before the bread is cooked through, 2 to 3 minutes, then flip and repeat on the other side.

4. Transfer the toasts to your plate and top with whatever you like before digging in!

"The Kids Are Sleeping Out" Chocolate Chip Cookie Brownie

I don't have kids, but I've met a child before so I know that when kids smell cookies or brownies, they immediately touch them with their sticky, germy little fingers and take rodent-size bites of all of them. This recipe is for a "brookie," which has a brownie bottom and chocolate chip cookie on top. It's perfect to make when your kids are out of the house—ideally when they're sleeping out, because your kitchen is going to smell awesome. If they find out you made this without them, it'll be a recurring issue in therapy for them in their thirties.

Makes 4 squares

Butter, for the pan

1 large egg

Brownie Batter

3 tablespoons unsalted butter, melted and cooled slightly

2 tablespoons unsweetened cocoa powder

2 tablespoons light brown sugar

1 tablespoon granulated sugar

¼ teaspoon pure vanilla extract

2 heaping tablespoons all-purpose flour

⅛ teaspoon kosher salt

Cookie Dough

2 tablespoons unsalted butter, melted and cooled slightly

1 tablespoon light brown sugar

1 tablespoon granulated sugar

¼ teaspoon pure vanilla extract

6 tablespoons all-purpose flour

⅛ teaspoon baking powder

⅛ teaspoon kosher salt

Pinch of baking soda

¼ cup semisweet chocolate chips

1. Preheat the oven to 350°F. Butter a 6½ × 5-inch baking dish, then line it with parchment paper, leaving some parchment overhanging two sides.

2. In a small measuring cup, whisk the egg until smooth and no streaks of egg white remain. You should have 4 tablespoons of egg.

3. **Make the brownie batter:** In a small bowl, stir together the melted butter and cocoa powder until smooth. Add the brown sugar and granulated sugar and stir until completely combined. Add the vanilla and measure out 3 tablespoons of the beaten egg, then stir until smooth. Add the flour and salt and fold them in with a spatula just until no streaks of flour remain. Spread the brownie batter into an even layer in the prepared pan.

4. **Make the cookie dough:** In another small bowl, combine the melted butter, brown sugar, and granulated sugar and stir until the mixture is fully incorporated. Pour in the remaining 1 tablespoon beaten egg and the vanilla and mix until smooth.

5. In another small bowl, mix the flour, baking powder, salt, and baking soda together with a fork. Add them to the butter mixture and stir it all together with the spatula just until no streaks of flour remain. Finally, fold in the chocolate chips.

6. Use your hands to gently press the cookie dough into a single, even layer the size of the baking pan. Place the dough over the brownie batter. Try to press the dough all the way to each corner, if you can, but do not mix the batter and dough. Cover the pan with aluminum foil.

7. Bake for 15 minutes, then uncover the pan and bake for 12 to 15 minutes more, until the cookie is golden brown and a toothpick inserted all the way to the bottom comes out with no wet brownie batter (try not to poke through a chocolate chip!). Transfer the baking dish to a wire rack and let the brookie cool in the pan until warm, about 20 minutes. Use the overhanging parchment to remove it from the pan, cut it into quarters, and eat.

The Small, Big Apple Pie

Do you know why New York is called the Big Apple? Me neither, so I looked it up, and it was not what I was expecting: "There are many apples on the success tree but when you pick New York City, you pick the Big Apple." This pie uses regular-size apples, and if you don't already have cloves, allspice, and nutmeg, no need to go buy them all—skipping one or two will still give you a delicious dessert that fits in your palm.

Serves 1 or 2

- 1 disk store-bought pie dough, thawed if necessary but kept cold
- 1/4 cup loosely packed light brown sugar
- 1 tablespoon all-purpose flour
- 1/2 teaspoon ground cinnamon
- 1/4 teaspoon kosher salt
- Pinch of ground cloves
- Pinch of ground allspice
- Pinch of ground nutmeg
- 2 small Granny Smith apples, peeled, cored, and cut into 1/4-inch-thick slices

Crumble Topping

- 1/4 cup all-purpose flour
- 3 tablespoons granulated sugar
- 1/4 teaspoon ground cinnamon
- 2 tablespoons unsalted butter, at room temperature

1. Preheat the oven to 400°F. You'll need a 6-inch round mini pie dish or a small (roughly 6½ × 5-inch) glass baking dish or metal baking pan.

2. Unroll the pie dough on your work surface. Gently drape it over your mini pie dish, easing it into the bottom corners and taking care to hold the edges gently so you don't pull it. Trim off all but 1 inch of overhanging dough around the edge. Fold the overhanging dough in and under itself, then use your thumb and index finger to crimp it, making sure the dough is pressed against the edge of the pie dish (this helps with shrinking). Prick the bottom a few times with a fork.

3. Line the dough with a piece of parchment paper or aluminum foil and fill it halfway to the top with either dried beans or uncooked rice. Bake for 10 minutes, then carefully remove the parchment and beans or rice and bake for 7 to 10 minutes more, until the bottom crust is dry and set. Remove the crust from the oven but keep the oven on.

4. Meanwhile, in a small bowl, combine the brown sugar, flour, cinnamon, salt, cloves, allspice, and nutmeg until evenly combined. Add the apples and toss to coat in the mixture.

5. **Make the crumble topping:** In a small bowl, mix the flour, granulated sugar, and cinnamon with your fingers. Add the butter and press the mixture together with your hands until the butter is incorporated, there is no dry flour left, and the mixture has formed into crumbles.

6. When the crust is ready, add the apple mixture, making sure there aren't any gaps. You want the apples to be *generously heaped*, not *precariously towered*. Depending on the dish you use and the size of your apples, you may need to hold back a few apple slices. Scatter the big crumbles of topping all over the top of the apples, then press any loose bits of the crumble mixture together to form more crumbles. Add it all to the top of the pie.

7. Bake for 20 minutes, then reduce the oven temperature to 350°F and bake for 15 to 20 minutes more, until you can hear the filling bubbling, the bottom crust is golden (if you can see it), and the apples are mostly tender (they'll keep softening as the pie cools). Transfer the baking dish to a wire rack and let cool completely before serving, about 2 hours.

My Little Croissant

I pity you if you've never seen the *Mad TV* sketch "Can I Have Your Number?" The actress Nicole Randall Johnson plays Darrel, an annoyingly persistent guy in a movie theater trying to get a woman's number, and it's art. It belongs in The Met. The sketch aired back in 2008 but still lives rent-free in my head. At one point, Darrel gives the woman he's pursuing the nickname "my little croissant." Now, *this* little croissant has a sweet almondy inside and buying almond extract is totally worth it. While the croissants bake, do yourself a favor and watch the sketch.

Makes 6 little croissants

1 large egg

1 tablespoon unsalted butter, at room temperature

2 tablespoons granulated sugar

½ teaspoon pure vanilla extract

⅛ teaspoon pure almond extract

¼ cup almond flour

1 teaspoon all-purpose flour

1 store-bought puff pastry sheet, thawed if necessary but kept cold

2 tablespoons sliced almonds

1. Line a baking sheet with parchment paper.

2. Crack the egg into a small measuring cup and beat until completely smooth and no streaks of egg white remain. You should have 4 tablespoons of egg.

3. In a small bowl, combine the butter and granulated sugar and press with your fingers until combined. Add 2 tablespoons of the egg, the vanilla, and the almond extract and whisk with a fork until smooth. Stir in the almond flour and all-purpose flour until combined.

4. Unroll the sheet of pastry; if it's a rectangle, position one of the shorter sides closest to you (if it's a square, doesn't matter). Cut the sheet lengthwise into thirds, so you have 3 long, skinny rectangles. Cut each rectangle diagonally to make 6 long, skinny triangles, each with a 90-degree angle in one corner, known as a "right triangle." Arrange the triangles so their bases are closest to you, then make a small (just ½-inch or so) slit along the short base. Use your hands to smooth and gently elongate the triangle, while also pulling the tip of the triangle to shape it from their original "right triangle" into a triangle with two equal sides and a sharp tip, also known as an "isosceles triangle" (geometry throwback!!).

5. Spread the almond mixture all over the triangles. Starting at the end with the slit, gently pull the corners away from each other to get the widest base possible, then roll all the way up toward the tip to form the croissant, continuing to pull the corners out to widen the croissant. Place it on the prepared baking sheet, with the tip on the bottom. Repeat with the other pieces of dough.

6. Transfer the baking sheet to the freezer or refrigerator (wherever there's room) and let it chill for 10 minutes. Preheat the oven to 350°F.

7. Add 1 teaspoon water to the remaining 2 tablespoons egg and mix. Brush the croissants with the egg wash and sprinkle with the almonds.

8. Bake for 40 to 45 minutes, until the croissants are deeply golden and crisp. Transfer them to a wire rack to cool until warm, about 15 minutes.

Cinnamon Rollin' with the Homies

In case there's any question or doubt, just because you're making single servings doesn't mean you're a friendless loser. I'm almost always cooking for myself, and I definitely have at least like four—no, *five*—friends . . . the exact number isn't important. If you wake up and you're feeling a little lonely, these cinnamon rolls can be shared with three homies who will be impressed no can was popped to produce them.

Makes 4 small rolls

8 ounces store-bought pizza dough

3 tablespoons unsalted butter, softened, sliced into 1-tablespoon pieces, plus more for greasing

All-purpose flour, for dusting

2 tablespoons light brown sugar

2 teaspoons ground cinnamon

⅛ teaspoon kosher salt

2 tablespoons full-fat cream cheese, at room temperature

¼ teaspoon pure vanilla extract

¼ cup powdered sugar

2 to 3 teaspoons whole milk (optional)

1. Pull the pizza dough from the fridge and let it sit at room temperature for 30 minutes. Preheat the oven to 350°F. Butter a small baking dish (I used my—you guessed it—6½ × 5-inch dish).

2. Lightly flour your work surface, rolling pin, and the dough. Roll the dough a few times horizontally, then a few times vertically, to start shaping it into a rectangle. Keep rolling and dusting the dough as needed, flipping every few rolls to keep it from sticking and keeping the sides as straight and the corners as square as possible, until it's 5 × 12 inches, with a shorter edge close to you.

3. In a small bowl, combine the brown sugar, cinnamon, and salt and mix with your fingers until fully combined. Spread 1 tablespoon of the butter all over the dough, leaving a ½-inch border on all sides except the one closest to you. Sprinkle the cinnamon mixture evenly over the butter.

4. Starting with the edge closest to you, roll the dough away from you, keeping the roll as even and tight as you can, until you've rolled all the way to the other end. Pinch the seam closed. Trim about ½ inch off each end and discard it, then slice the roll of dough crosswise into four 1-inch-thick pieces. Place them cut-side down and evenly spaced in the baking pan. Let the rolls rise at room temperature, uncovered, for 10 minutes, to puff up slightly. Cut 1 tablespoon of the butter into 4 small pieces and put one on top of each roll.

5. Bake for about 25 minutes, until the rolls are puffed up and cooked through. Remove from the oven and let cool until they're just warm, about 15 minutes.

Recipe continues

6. Meanwhile, in a small bowl, combine the remaining 1 tablespoon butter, the cream cheese, and the vanilla and mix until smooth and combined. Add the powdered sugar and mix again until smooth. If you'd like a thinner frosting, add milk 1 teaspoon at a time and stir until it's your ideal consistency.

7. Spread the cream cheese frosting on top of the warm rolls and enjoy.

What to do if the homies are running late: Freeze the rolls after they rise and when your guests arrive pop the rolls in the oven. If they're really late, when they finally show just microwave each for 10 to 15 seconds before serving—and remind yourself why eating alone is sometimes the best.

The Fellowship of the Lemon Ricotta Pancake

Out of all the recipes I've ever made, the most infuriatingly absurdly large is always a pancake recipe. Whenever I follow one, I end up with the same number of pancakes as there were extras in a *Lord of the Rings* movie. I don't want that, and neither do you, which brings us to the One Recipe to Rule Them All. The tang of the buttermilk mixes well with the tang from the lemon and will lift you sky-high, but the ricotta will bring you back down to Middle Earth. This will give you a nice stack of two or three precious mini pancakes.

Serves 1

1 lemon

1 tablespoon granulated sugar

3 tablespoons whole-milk ricotta cheese, stirred

2 tablespoons buttermilk or whole milk

¼ teaspoon pure vanilla extract

3 tablespoons all-purpose flour

⅛ teaspoon baking powder

⅛ teaspoon kosher salt

1 large egg, separated

1 tablespoon unsalted butter

Powdered sugar, for dusting

Maple syrup, for serving

1. Run the lemon over a Microplane or other fine grater twice so you zest about a quarter of it into a small bowl. Cut the un-zested half of the lemon into wedges and set aside for serving. Add the granulated sugar to the bowl with the lemon zest and rub them together with your fingers until well combined—this will give you a better lemony taste. Stir in the ricotta, buttermilk, and vanilla until smooth. Add the flour, baking powder, and salt to the ricotta mixture and gently stir until combined but a few lumps remain. Don't overmix here!

2. Place the egg white in a medium bowl. Whisk the egg white until it's white, it has doubled in volume, and is starting to stiffen up, 1 to 2 minutes. Add the batter and gently fold everything together, preserving as much of the air you whisked into the egg white as possible.

3. Melt the butter in a medium or large cast-iron skillet over medium-low heat. When the butter is foaming, swirl it around to evenly coat the pan. Use a ¼-cup measure to portion the batter into the pan, fitting as many pancakes as you can without them touching. Cook until the edges are set and bubbles form in the center of the pancake, adjusting the heat if the bottom is browning too much before the edges are set, 2 to 3 minutes. Flip the pancakes and cook until golden on the second side and cooked through, 1 to 2 minutes more. Transfer the pancakes to a plate and repeat with the remaining batter if necessary.

4. When you have your stack of pancakes, dust them with as much powdered sugar as you like and squeeze a lemon wedge over the top before enjoying with maple syrup.

Oh my God, Becky, look at her manuscript. It is *so* big. It looks like one of those rap guy's girlfriend's manuscripts!!!

Well, here it is—my cookbook. This was a passion project of mine, and there are SO many people I need to give my firstborn to in order to properly thank them for their time, their support, their energy, and their belief that this could actually happen. In order of operations . . .

Thank you to my team at CAA—thank you to Olivia Blaustein (and Brigitte) for not laughing at me when I said I wanted to do a cookbook, and for introducing me to my book agent, Anthony Mattero. Thank you, Anthony (and Sydney), for not laughing at me when I said I wanted to do a cookbook. Thank you for introducing me to the world's best publishing team, my editors at Union Square & Co., Caitlin Leffel and Amanda Englander: I had so many questions (because I'm not a professional chef), and your patience and intelligence are a rare and much appreciated gift.

Thank you to Ghazalle and her incredible team—Bridget, Megan, Ann, Barrett, and Alexis—for capturing the joy of cooking for one so beautifully. I'm grateful for your good vibes and endless patience and for turning every dish into a celebration. And thank you for being so incredibly kind to Peanut, who probably should've been on anti-anxiety meds.

Thank you to the countless friends and neighbors who ate the food I could not and gave feedback on recipes and headnotes, and a particularly special shout-out to the friends who did a round of testing for me because I can't eat anything spicy. ☺ The biggest thanks to Maddie Boardman, Scott Ritter, Shivani Banker, Anthony Zych, Jessica Goodman, Maxwell Strachan, Cecelia Worthington, Sonia Kharkar, Alisa Singer, David Elfman, and Flora Greeson.

This book would literally have never happened without the skill, talent, and genius of the professional cooks who helped me build this world, Ali Slagle and Emily Stephenson. Ali was instrumental in putting together the proposal and sample recipes, while Emily (ahoy!) tested and developed the rest of the book. I'd probably be dead without Emily, who is so incredibly patient. If I were her, I would've killed me halfway through the cheesy chapter. ☺

Thank you to my family for faking your belief that I could do this; that was very supportive of you. It takes a village to . . . well, no one actually finishes that sentence, but it really takes a village to build something great, and thanks to the people mentioned, I know this book is great.

Note: Page references in *italics* indicate photographs.

D

E

F

G

P

T

V

W